8' X 30' ~ TO PLANT AND REPEAT

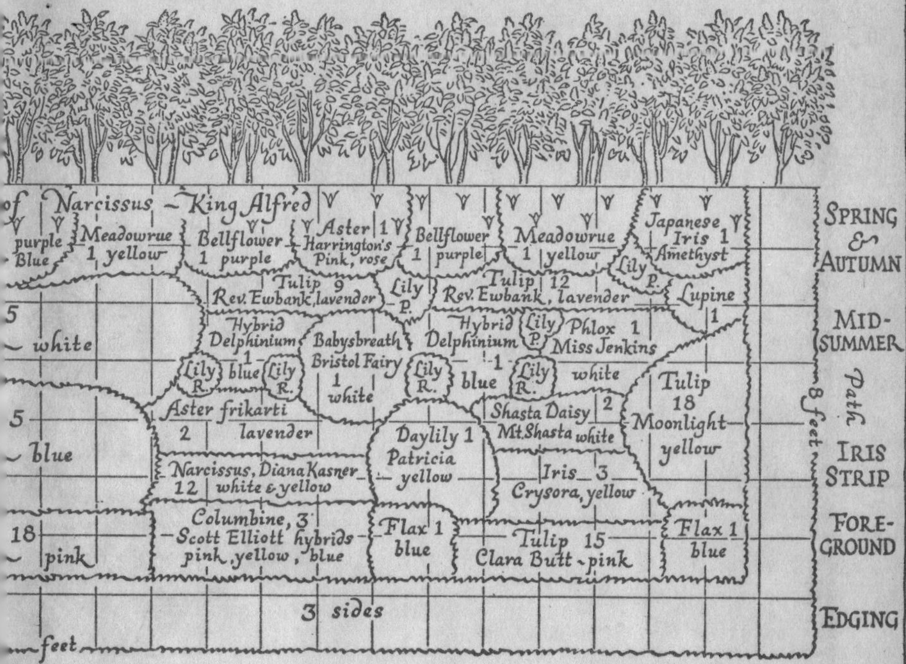

2.25

As space permits, white nicotiana seedlings fill tulip areas in rear; ruffled white petunias, Snowstorm Improved, are planted along front; and end tulip spaces carry pink petunias, Cheerful. Single plants of marigold, Yellow Supreme, are set along the back next the peony and Japanese iris plants. Narcissus area at rear is covered by the perennials growing there. Narcissus areas in foreground are planted with snapdragon, Yellow Giant.

PERENNIALS PREFERRED

In this June garden, with its distant vista of hills, perennials are pleasantly colonized along the winding course of a little stream.

PERENNIALS PREFERRED

By
Helen Van Pelt Wilson

Drawings by Kathleen Voute

M. BARROWS & COMPANY, INC.
PUBLISHERS NEW YORK

FIRST PRINTING

PRINTED IN THE UNITED STATES OF AMERICA
AMERICAN BOOK–STRATFORD PRESS, INC., NEW YORK

FOR MY HUSBAND

Ralph B. Umsted

A MASTER BUILDER OF COLD FRAMES

ACKNOWLEDGMENT

FOR assistance in the preparation of this book sincere thanks are first due to Dorothy H. Jenkins. I am also grateful for the critical reading of various chapters or for other help to John C. Wister, R. C. Allen, Eleanor G. Ritter, Elizabeth G. Henny, Harry Candy, Isabel B. Fasel, Frances C. Gaskill, Edith Stokes Haines, Katherine G. Bary, Mary Jacobsen, Paul F. Frese, Patricia Spollen and to The Pennsylvania Horticultural Society. The flower arrangements have been made by Anne B. Wertsner and Mrs. William Stickles. Appreciation is likewise expressed to *The New York Times, House Beautiful, House and Garden, Better Homes & Gardens* and *The Home Garden* since the subject matter of certain chapters has been used in articles previously written for these publications.

Quotations from copyrighted poems appearing in this book are used by permission of and special arrangements with:

Harper & Brothers for "God's World" in *Renascence & Other Poems*, Copyright, 1917, by Edna St. Vincent Millay; Charles Scribner's Sons for the quotations from Cosmo Monkhouse and Katharine Tynan; Little, Brown & Company for the selections from *The Robin* and *Psalm of the Day*, both by Emily Dickinson; Dodd, Mead & Company for *Green Fingers* by Reginald Arkell, Copyright, 1936; Houghton Mifflin Company for "September Days" in *Poems* by George Arnold, and for "December" by Christopher P. Cranch in *The Bird And The Bell*; L. C. Page & Company for "An April Adoration" by Charles G. D. Roberts.

CONTENTS

LIST OF ILLUSTRATIONS

❧ ❧

FOREWORD

MY GARDEN IS A CITADEL

PERENNIAL—through the years. How pleasant to me is the intrinsic meaning of this word characterizing the many lovely flowers which through the years have afforded me both solace and joy. Recalling childhood, I have no memories earlier than those of our garden where spicy old-fashioned pinks, early peonies, scented August lilies and dark pungent chrysanthemums marked the passing seasons. More sturdy and fragrant than many flowers we grow today, they were often less handsome, but still dearly loved by the child who also "played store" with canna seeds, sucked nectar from honeysuckle tubes and with daisies made a crown for her little sister's head.

We who have early known gardens intimately have a most precious heritage. Not only do they afford us an ever delightful and rewarding occupation but as time unfolds, our love for gardening proves a bulwark against life. In happy years we women consider our garden simply as part of our homemaking. We design them as outside living or dining rooms with sky for ceiling, grass for floor and encompassing walls of evergreens or flowering shrubs. They are background for summer parties or the setting for great family events like weddings or anniversary celebrations. We plant in them a wealth of flowers for bouquets to blend with the wallpaper in the hall or draperies in the library.

But to all of us come times when our gardens are much more than this pleasant attribute of good living. My garden is a citadel where I turn to unravel intricate matters or seek valor to face crisis or sorrow. For a garden never fails the one who plans and tends it. The night after my young sister's death it was the tall grandeur of the lilies and the splendid blue verticals of the delphinium which alleviated the anguish of my spirit. The first moon she will never see, I thought. But even the impact of that terrible finality was eased by a vivid, mystical assurance that now her beauty was merged with the loveliness of these scented moonlit flowers.

A garden always welcomes us whether we return from a journey or an illness. I recall a June I never saw my garden. But I did enjoy its background when the first day I sat up I found my window framing a new picture of the peach orchard richly carpeted in purple vetch. The next year I missed June again. This time it seemed not to matter until one day my nurse broke off a stalk of a lily. What a regal rattle of enamel and gold Benvenuto Cellini might have made with such a model, I thought, only my new daughter will prefer the original. So I hastened to recover and show her her first lilies before they faded for the year.

Often in my garden I have experienced the incomparable joy of an hour or a season's climax of grace. When in autumn, masses of chrysanthemums have gleamed like a fallen sunset against a blue, cloud-driven sky I have felt the pressure of beauty beyond bearing and cried out with Millay,

> "Lord, I do fear
> Thou'st made the world too beautiful this year;
> My soul is all but out of me,—let fall
> No burning leaf; prithee, let no bird call."

But essentially it is the doing in a garden rather than the seeing which is dearest to us all. It is our close preoccupation with the timeless verities of seed and soil which yields both peace and delight. For seed sowing is an act of faith. The cultivation of the soil is creative and the gathering and giving of flowers grown by ourselves deeply gratifying.

When my dear Louise protests, "It ain't fittin', you like that in the afternoon and the Mister, he comin' in any minute. You should be a settin' on that bench with some sewin'. Look at them knees. It just ain't fittin'."

"You're right, Louise," I admit, "but don't scold me. On the outside I'm a sight. I know it. But you should see what a clean and shining spirit I have within."

Germantown, 1944.

PERENNIALS PREFERRED

CHAPTER I

FIRST PRINCIPLES FOR PERENNIAL BORDERS

PERENNIALS are plants with many values. Yet more often than not we entirely overlook their simple landscape possibilities and place them in herbaceous borders. This is the most complex arrangement of all but the loveliest, it is true, when attractive color harmonies are achieved for each season. Frequently, however, disappointments occur because we expect of our perennials continuous bloom and eternal life.

Like people, perennials have their limitations. Until we allow for these, while emphasizing all their glorious assets, we can never create pictures which quite suit us. We must eventually admit, therefore, that a satisfactory border starts not with seeds, soil or plants but with the gardener's state of mind. It is, in fact, an exercise in evaluation.

I found this out two decades ago when I made my first border. I was greener then than the greenest plant I grew for I had no real information about perennials. I just loved them all and wanted for myself every variety I discovered. I was a one-of-each gardener trying to create a paradise from my neighbors' cast-offs.

Today I attempt less than in that first garden, yet I achieve far more. For now I apply to the making of a garden certain definite rules. I pass these principles on to you after repeated tests of their soundness.

I. First, provide a strong background. Perennials cannot stand alone. They require a setting.

If you have ever planted free-standing borders you know what a thin appearance they make. Sometimes, to be sure, the site of the garden requires this and you must get the best effect you can. In such emergency plant the tall, late-flowering varieties of hardy aster along the back of your border. Hollyhocks, meadowrue and other tall subjects which must be cut down after early blooming are not so satisfactory.

Much more happily situated is the perennial border with a green hedge of yew behind it or a stalwart line of shrubs. Where possible I have planted double white lilacs as background for my borders and find their enduring green excellent while their scented flowering makes twice blessed the lavender pink and yellow pageant of May perennials.

The mixed shrubbery boundary of small properties also provides a pleasing backdrop. Let the outline of your perennial borders follow its curves and bays and you will have charming pictures. A house wall, too, may be considered but dividing walls of brick or stone such as the English use are the ideal setting. Such walls are, of course, the goal of us all in our affluent years.

After the site is chosen, next consider the plants.

II. In selecting perennials for a border emphasize the reliables. Eliminate those which bloom briefly, sulk after flowering or are unduly rampant. Peonies, iris, delphinium, phlox, hardy asters and perhaps early chrysanthemums are worthy of leading roles. Let columbines, flax, candytuft, meadowrue and such play the secondary parts. Omit entirely in limited spaces bleedinghearts, oriental poppies and other perennials which disappear completely after flowering. And think twice about admitting hardy ageratum, beebalm or heleniums which are of far too exuberant a nature for restricted areas.

III. Proceed by plan only. Plant your perennials on paper before you put them in soil.

DIGGING ON PAPER IS EASIER.

Through the winter think out your border design. Work and rework it by drawings. Even then you will be tempted to make yearly changes in the actualities. A good plan, however, saves a lot of useless effort and makes planting easier too. You can work your schemes out on graph paper, filling in the sections with crayons to test your color harmonies. Or you can just rule a large piece of plain paper into guiding squares. Well-illustrated catalogues will acquaint you with the look of unfamiliar perennials. The Cultural Index on page 197 will inform you as to heights, colors and seasons.

IV. As you plan, strive for emphasis throughout the garden by repeating drifts or colonies of the same plants. Place also the same single specimens at regular intervals for accent.

Such repetition gives a garden picture unity and strength. If the layout of the beds can also be balanced, that too helps considerably. In my present garden, I have two long borders on each side of a wide grass panel. Three beds are planted exactly alike while the fourth varies somewhat in the center because it is shaded by an ancient apple tree. Yet I find no monotony in this small garden, only that pleasant restful result which orderly planting produces. The smaller the garden the more essential to effect is such repetition and emphasis. You will find that while two peonies, three hardy asters or four flax plants carelessly scattered in an undesigned border say very little, evenly spaced through four beds or through a long border, composed of repeated units, they produce a real harmony.

V. From the start make your flower beds as wide as their setting permits. Let them measure one-third more than the height of the tallest plant they are to contain. Otherwise your important background giants will balance precariously.

Wide beds are essential to rich effects. Even with eight-by-thirty-foot sections like mine it takes careful planning to get a fairly continuous parade of flowers. With the often attempted three-foot beds a varied effect is impossible. It is better to give over such narrow spaces to one season. Select peonies, for example, for the main show and edge the bed with tulips followed by petunias. You will not then attempt more in narrow limits than you can successfully achieve. And spring will be handsome while summer is pleasant.

If you want greater variety in plants, beds must be deep. They must be wide enough, in fact, to hold one mass of plants which will burst into bloom as another quiets down. Perhaps, too, some groups must be included to hide the complete retirement of others, Chinese delphinium before oriental poppies, for example. In my eight-foot sections you will notice that I manage a five-deep line-up. That is little enough planting depth when the aim is continuous color. A ten-foot bed would simplify the task. (See front end paper.)

Let me emphasize, however, that although my garden usually seems in full bloom it really is not. To be sure, there is practically always some color but not nearly as much as appears on four crescendo occasions. In April, in May, in late June and again before frost there is truly a glowing spectacle. Three or four such occasions in one garden are all that can be expected. Between times the effect is necessarily quiet. But excellent color is always enhanced by a balanced design of beds and by good foliage on plants out of bloom.

VI. Consider, therefore, the leaves as well as the flower of every perennial you select for your border.

At first I never thought of the looks of a plant out of bloom. Now dependable foliage seems to me as important as long flowering. Therefore I stress the evergreen hardy candytuft and iris, and in the border usually forego bleedinghearts and Virginia bluebells, much as I admire them. With such perennials, there is an unattractive period when foliage is maturing and on the yellow side, and again when it actually disappears and the gardener beholds not flowers, nor leaves, but just bare ground. It is better, therefore, to rely on plants which look well both in and out of bloom. Of these there is a multitude—peonies, iris, daylilies, meadowrue, pinks, baptisia and gas plant for a start. Enduring foliage is particularly important for all edging plants.

VII. In general, plan for the color in your perennial border to start in spring at the rim and move to the rear as the season proceeds. Think of your design as composed of five not too well-defined strips. Call these arbitrarily the Edging, Foreground, Iris, Midsummer and Autumn Stratas.

This is a suggestive principle, not an ironclad rule. You may, if you wish, use late dwarf asters for the edging or set a peony or so, as I do, along the rear. You can interrupt The Iris Strip with summer shasta daisies or place spring meadowrue in your autumn background. Experience indicates many such pleasing variations. Consider, however, seasonal differences in heights. I used to place delphinium at the very back. Now with its shorter second and third bloomings in mind, I keep it forward with tall phlox beside rather than before it.

VIII. Finally, to make the most of your border plantings, keep them neat.

Good grooming, you will discover, does as much for an out-of-bloom garden as it does for a plain woman. Therefore through the less vivid weeks cultivate your garden faithfully and keep it sharply edged and firmly staked. Divide your plants every three years or so to hold them within the confines you first selected. Sometimes discard them entirely and begin afresh. Perennials often live many years but not forever. You can not achieve a neat and finished effect with any but first quality material.

Here then, briefly, are your guiding principles to handsome perennial borders.

I. Provide a background.
II. Give leading roles to the big five—Iris, Peony, Delphinium, Phlox and Hardy Aster.
III. Proceed by plan only.
IV. Emphasize and repeat.
V. Design wide borders.
VI. Consider foliage as well as flower.
VII. Arrange color in a front to rear wave.
VIII. Keep your borders neat.

At this point I wish I could offer an absolutely satisfactory plan for a perennial border unit with a few annuals and bulbs introduced for supplementary color. But I have discovered that no one else's plan is ever quite right. Only you can evaluate your own factors, estimate the time you can give to culture and decide what plants are indispensable. I include, therefore, a sketch of my own plan (see front end paper) not for you to copy, but just to illustrate these essential principles which I have learned through many happy years of garden experience.

Notice in this scheme the four crescendos. The first one occurs in late April and early May when the snowy candytuft edging blooms with rear and mid-lines of yellow narcissus. These together sing a lovely spring song.

Then in May and early June a second voice arises paralleling the first for a time like themes in Bach's fugues. Yellow, pink and lavender tulips bloom now with blue and gold iris, azure flax, *Linum*, lemon daylilies, *Hemerocallis*, and pastel columbines, *Aquilegia.* (The tulips and narcissus bulbs are planted eight to ten inches deep so that seedling annuals can later be set among them and cultivated through the summer without harm to the bulbs below.)

The theme of early summer is next carried by the blue delphinium, yellow meadowrue, *Thalictrum*, purple bellflowers, *Campanula*, and white babysbreath, *Gypsophila*, Lingard phlox and regal lilies. Soon after these comes the white phlox, Mrs. Jenkins, and the amethyst *Iris kaempferi.*

There will not be another crescendo now until autumn

but mid-summer will still have its music. The phlox varieties, bellflowers, babysbreath and flax will flower intermittently while yellow zinnias transplanted from the cold frame replace the forward narcissus colonies. (Perennials soon conceal the bulb foliage along the back line.) The tulips will be covered by large-flowering petunias, white Snowstorm Improved and pink Cheerful, which the florist starts for me in the greenhouse late in February. And through the beds will spring up everywhere white and fragrant flowering tobacco, *Nicotiana affinis*. This takes over all unexpectedly empty spaces.

Such a self-sowing annual is a fine addition to the perennial border. Perhaps you may prefer cornflowers or larkspur in yours. All you need do is sow any one of them once—nicotiana in spring, the other two in October—and they are yours for life. You must, however, be firm with these spring volunteers and not let enough remain to encroach on space belonging to delphinium or phlox.

In September bursts the fourth crescendo. Then tall blue asters and white philippinense lilies sound the final theme. These merge into the long continuing melody which began in April and is only silenced by frost.

As for color, I do not attempt unusual or subtle harmonies. Perhaps you will prefer stronger tones than those of my pastel borders with their white emphasis. But where summers are very hot a white and green symphony appears pleasant and cool even on torrid days and, of course, pale flowers tend to be more scented than others.

Furthermore, in twilight and moonlight it is the frosty lily, the ivory phlox and the white satin petunia which still remain visible in the darkness. To us and our visiting city friends their evening beauty affords gentle solace of spirit through trying summer weeks. And this is, indeed, the rewarding joy of a garden.

❦ ❦

CHAPTER II

THE ABC OF SOILS, COMPOST AND FERTILIZERS

TOO many of us have started gardening with seed packets. That's like concentrating on wall paper and forgetting about the cellar. In gardens, as in houses, good foundations count, and a friable and fertile soil is the only sound basis for a beautiful garden. But to condition your soil so that it will afford a comfortable medium for the sustenance of plant roots is not always a simple matter.

First you must understand what you are after. What is meant, for example, by those terms friable and fertile, so freely scattered about in print? A friable soil has water-holding capacity. It is well aerated and easily penetrated by plant roots. Because of its humus content it is rich in active bacteria. A fertile soil is plentifully supplied with those elements which are necessary to the healthy, balanced growth of plants. Bacteria present in a friable soil make the elements of fertility readily available to plants. A soil lacking humus can be rich but still not a good growing medium because the fertile elements, failing bacterial action, are locked away and inert.

Soil must be not only of first quality but also deeply prepared, at least to eighteen inches for perennial borders. Then, unless you are certain drainage is good, as on a sloping site, dig a bit more and place a six-inch layer of stones and debris in the bottom for drainage purposes. Next, take pains to improve the soil which chance has given you. The first year, if most of the garden budget goes into the hiring of a digger and the purchasing of unromantic but reliable soil-conditioning materials, it is all to the good. So prepared for, the future advent of gorgeous blooms is assured. If you work vice versa you will be eternally frustrated by losses due to rot from standing water or fatigued by more cultivating than a better prepared soil would require.

Lime

After spading, consider the advisability of a soil test. But do not imitate the routine practice of many gardeners who follow digging with liming. The indiscriminate use of lime is dangerous policy since lime is neither cure-all nor fertilizer but only a means of altering the pH of the soil. Sometimes the pH of a soil is just fine as it is and changing it means doing something you must later undo. Incidentally pH is a term describing the sweet-sour condition of the soil, the way Fahrenheit readings indicate hot-cold degrees of temperature.

Most perennials thrive in a fairly neutral or pH 7 soil with toleration for slight variations either way. You can determine the pH of your own particular plot only by test. This you can manage yourself by means of a simple chemical home testing kit or you can send a soil sample to your county agent. For a small fee he will make the necessary analysis and recommendation.

The sandy or clayey consistency of soil and its humus content are further determining factors. So don't follow blindly any general advice about adding so many pounds of lime per square foot of flower bed. This is no kindness to your perennials.

Generally speaking apply lime (1) to sweeten sour soils (2) to produce a definitely alkaline condition, reading above pH 7 for plants like delphinium, gypsophila, carnation and pink which seems to prefer a sweet growing medium (3) to correct over-rich conditions due to too frequent applications of manure and (4) to exert a slightly disinfecting action where soil-borne diseases have been prevalent and where nematodes frequently attack peonies and chrysanthemums.

Lime the soil when it is necessary at least two weeks ahead of fertilizing, never at the same time since lime tends to free food elements faster than perennials can assimilate them. This results in waste. Late autumn is propitious for liming since other garden work slows down then and fertilizing is over for the season.

Humus

Next, consider the consistency of the soil and its humus content. A garden cannot be made by scratching the earth and applying fertilizer. Foods are important to be sure, but they are beneficial only when their medium of operation is a soil rich in humus. Humus is partially decomposed organic or once living matter. It improves a clayey soil by opening it up and making it porous. It corrects a thin sandy one by giving it bulk and some capacity for holding water. But the greatest value of humus lies in its supply of bacteria which, operating in the soil, makes available to plant roots elements otherwise useless.

For gardens not yet on a self-running basis, either commercially available humus or peat moss is excellent. Peat moss corrects the mechanical ills of the soil and increases bacterial action. It supplies soil sponges for retaining water. In fact, it holds about ten times its dry weight in moisture. When beds are newly dug, enough is added by bulk to give the soil a crumbly consistency if a handful of it is squeezed.

Other sources of humus are mushroom compost and the readily available and excellent shredded and pulverized manures. Well-rotted, that means two-year-old, horse or cow manure from a farm is still perhaps the best soil conditioner there is, though of slight fertilizing value. Leaf mold, of course, is fine. In time, however, a garden should become self-sufficient and produce a large quantity of its own humus through the conservation of leaves and other vegetable material collected and rotted down via the compost heap or pit. Personally, I could not manage a garden without at least one and better three compost pits.

Compost

I prefer pits to heaps because there are few out-of-sight spots in my garden. My compost pits are, therefore, dug three by six by four feet deep and the sides lined with old porch floor boards. Into their roomy depths go in the course of summer and fall most of the garden debris—grass clippings, leaves, vegetable tops (but not corn stalks) and faded bouquets. A sprinkling of lime or of Adco to hasten decomposition and a thin layer of soil, sods or sand is more or less systematically cast over each twelve-inch layer of refuse until the top of the pit is reached.

The surface then is not flattened off, but hollowed a little to catch the rain water. This hastens decomposition. In addition, the pit is soaked monthly through the summer for a whole day by a full-tilt hose. With some two or three turnings in the course of the season on days when other work is almost caught up, this material is thoroughly mingled. Within a twelve to eighteen-month period most of it has reached that pleasant, crumbly condition so dear to the experienced gardener's heart. By keeping two pits going, there is always one about ready for use and one on the way. Three, of course, with one just for leaves is pure luxury. Both maple and oak leaves may be included, so don't worry over the sweet and sour soil problem here.

Gardeners who work on a small scale will find that even the behind-a-shrub compost heap, small though it be, has value. With a spreading spirea as a screen, perhaps, scoop out a wide circle of soil, six to twelve inches deep. Around this stake a retentive ten to twelve-foot strip of woven wire and into the area throw the garden refuse, except, of course, infected or pest-carrying stalks. Here, too, time will produce several wheelbarrow loads of humus.

Fertility

To keep your garden richly supplied with basic plant nutrients you need to know something of its requirements. Plants must have nitrogen to promote leaf and stem strength and to stimulate growth generally. When there is too much, they grow prodigiously, but in spindly fashion and are poor flower producers. Witness the too-thin delphinium plants with small florets of sickly bloom or the sappy growth of overfed phlox. Obviously, however, plants emphasizing leaf growth like baptisia, can do with a lot of nitrogen.

Phosphorus is for roots. It also gives a steady push to flower and seed production. With too little phosphorus, foliage lacks color. With too much, it is sappy, lacking fiber, and weak so that plants require a lot of staking.

Potash, the third essential element, is the antotoxin among plant foods. It wards off disease, stabilizes growth, and intensifies color. A plant suffering from a lack of it is dull and sickly looking. But if it has too much, it may make false growth, which afterwards will fall over.

The amounts of these three basic elements are marked on the bags and cartons of the various trade-marked brands of complete plant foods in numbered series like 5-8-5, 4-12-4, 6-7-3, etc. The first number always represents the proportion of nitrogen content, the second the phosphate, and the third the potash. In addition, mention may be made of the presence of certain "trace elements"—iron, boron or manganese—which in small quantities are also necessary to healthy plant life.

All-Purpose Foods

When buying a commercial plant food, read the label carefully and try to select one on which it is plainly indicated that some of the nitrogen is from organic or once-living material. These organic elements will be less quickly available and hence have a more lasting value than those which the greedy plant can consume all at once. For regular use I am partial to a 6-8-5 plant food "with not less than sixty percent of the nitrogen derived from organic sources," but I have, too, a purely chemical 4-12-4 mix for spring and summer stimulation. With this, plants need in fall some rotted manure or organic bone meal as supplementary food.

As a general thing apply commercial plant foods to perennials about April 15 and again on May 15 in sufficient quantity slightly to obscure the soil. Do this just before you cultivate. Then after you have worked it in well, water deeply, unless you are lucky enough to catch a rain.

Avoid mixing plant foods with the soil in which seeds are to be sown. Also, if seedlings are transplanted, and not just thinned out, wait until growth has commenced before applying fertilizer. These all-purpose foods often act faster than such young plants can tolerate.

Manures

Special feeding and stimulation does not, of course, take the place of proper soil preparation before planting. If you live in the country and have natural manures available, your procedure can include less buying. By adding peat moss to the poultry runs you can obtain a fertile humus material. Collect this but, before use, compost it for six months under cover of old burlap bags but with the sides of the stack exposed. A good plan is to make alternate layers of four inches of the manure and one inch of commercial superphosphate. The urea will thus be absorbed and the superphosphate cause quick rotting.

When horse or cow manure is available, pile it in the open without cover for at least one year. Two years are better. Then dig it into the flower beds when they are first prepared and supplement with a top dressing of some complete fertilizer since manure is, as I have said, a soil conditioner rather than a plant food.

With some such soil-building program, your garden will grow on the finest of foundations. It will require of you a minimum of upkeep. It will even produce that beauty your optimism and the seed catalogues have led you to expect.

CHAPTER III

THE COMFORTS OF MOISTURE AND MULCH

WHEN your perennials have been planted in carefully devised soil, they can stand well the heat and drought of summer, especially if cultivation is constant and what the old hands call a "dust mulch" is maintained. A dust mulch consists of a fine loose condition of the top inch or so of soil. When this is worked up regularly, particularly after each rain, weeds, discouraged in infancy, do not mature to spoil the garden's looks and feed upon its resources. Furthermore, a pleasantly cool and moist condition is maintained around the roots.

But how many of us have time or vigor to keep a dust mulch in operation? More generally useful, therefore, is the applied mulch through which weeds seldom intrude and from which soil moisture does not evaporate. A number of good mulching materials may be purchased. Shredded redwood fiber is one you will do well to consider. This material, fine enough for water to pass directly through, is still so tough it disintegrates slowly. Therefore it may be gathered up between seasons and used for several years. If your soil is heavy, spread it an inch deep. Allow two inches on sandy soils. Buckwheat hulls are another possibility.

But my favorite mulch is the blessed peat moss of which I have never, never had enough. The horticultural grade is the kind I like for its just-right degree of coarseness. If a two-inch layer of this is spread in mid-June over the entire garden just after it has been well cultivated and watered, how exquisitely neat it stays through the summer heat and how very comfortable it appears to feel. The gardener is comfortable too. She has then only the most occasional weed to pull and in the heat she can contentedly rock on the porch without being reproached by the terrible urgency of an unkempt border.

This peat moss may in fall or spring be worked into the soil. It thus adds beneficially to the organic content there. But if a very thick layer has been used and the expense has been unpleasantly noticeable, the peat moss mulch is not worked in at all but scraped up and stored in baskets for next summer's spreading.

Before applying it to your borders, moisten it thoroughly. Dry peat moss spread on dry soil can be a detriment unless there is an immediate heavy rainfall. After ripping off the top and bottom strip of burlap and removing much of the packing, stand a new bale outside where rain will reach it. Or place a slow-running hose in the center and let it go until the peat moss has absorbed as much moisture as possible. Since a standard bale contains eighteen to twenty-two bushels, you can obtain from it an inch-deep mulch for two hundred and fifty to three hundred square feet of bed. I think so well of peat moss, indeed, that I regularly put it on my Christmas list along with my annual request for a load of manure, my favorite present, but, alas, one I have been able to achieve but once, my family not considering it suitable for greetings of the season.

Some mulches can also be produced right in the garden. Fairly fine leaf mold from your compost pit does not look so well as peat moss, perhaps, but it does the job and is also richly nutritious, which peat moss is not. Grass clippings, if applied gradually, a thin layer at a time with opportunity to dry thoroughly before additions are made, are also suitable.

Watering

Although mulching conserves moisture there still are times of prolonged drought in summer which necessitates extra watering. When these occur, be thorough. Even if your husband adores it and it soothes and quiets him in hot weather, don't give him the hose to play with in the evening.

Nothing is worse for a garden than a regular evening sprinkle. It encourages surface instead of deep rooting of perennials and is an out-and-out invitation to a number of blights and diseases because foliage then goes into the darkness wet and fungous spores can thus make a field day of the night. Morning and late afternoons are the best times to water, but not nearer than two hours to sunset. Blazing midday and early afternoon are not good. But if you are doing the job thoroughly it will not matter if the sun shines on the foliage at the same time that the sprinkler is running.

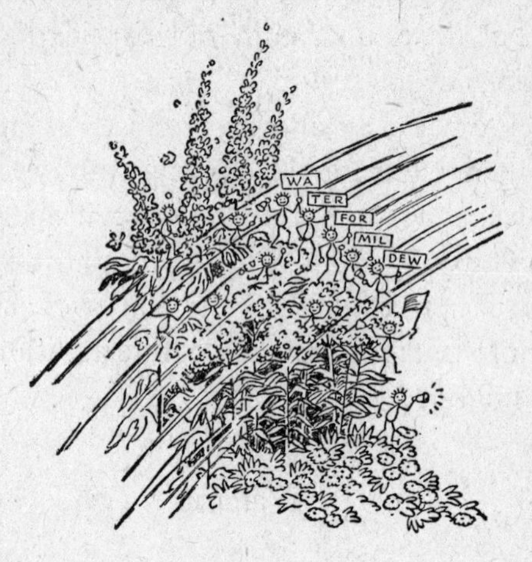

The best way to soak roots deeply, of course, is not to use a sprinkler but to draw a slow-running hose among peonies or phlox or into the midst of the border. If the nozzle is laid on a narrow board this will prevent washing. Let the water run about an hour in each area. You will be surprised if you examine the soil in less time to see how little of it has been reached. At least six inches is your goal.

A porous canvas tube called a soil soaker makes deep, thorough watering a less exacting task than the nozzle-on-board system. This soaker, which can be attached to your hose, comes in twelve to fifty-foot lengths. Select a length nearest that of your longest bed. Extensive sections in a small garden are clumsy because water backs up in the soaker if you have to bend it.

Sometimes, of course, you will need to use a rotating sprinkler which projects a fine mist over a long distance.

NEVER LET YOUR HUSBAND PLAY WITH THE HOSE IN THE EVENING.

This overhead method taking the place of rainfall covers a wide section of garden without puddling soil and without requiring much attention from you. And it does afford great refreshment to plant tops on a hot day.

Incidentally, if the autumn tends to be dry, give your garden a thorough final soaking in late October or early November. Then plant roots will go into the winter plump and healthy. Plants left thirsty in autumn are always likely to winterkill.

Winter Covering

As for winter protection, the final matter of plant contentment to be considered, don't overdo it. Around Philadelphia and, indeed, in many other places especially where gardens are hedged in considerably, very little is needed. Indeed, for some years now I have not covered my garden at all and my losses seem slight.

The aim in covering or mulching at this season, is, of course, to prevent that alternate freezing and thawing of the soil which our fluctuating climate induces. The summer mulch is used to conserve moisture and insulate the soil against extreme heat but the winter mulch is applied to keep the cold in and the frozen condition constant. Persisting snow is a natural mulch. So, too, are leaves. And this is the one for most of us to rely on unless the luxury of a two- to three-inch winter layer of peat moss is possible. Peat moss, I may say, certainly does look well for on-view beds near the house.

Many leaves naturally collect, however, and catch among the crowns of the plants in the perennial border (the tall tops are, of course, cut down before mulching). But more leaves usually have to be added to get a uniform distribution. Any leaves will do except those of the poplars and Norway maples which mat down like soggy rags and exclude all air from the plants while pressing dampness down upon them all winter long. Oak, birch, hickory, beech, linden and the hardwood maples are fine. Indeed, any leaves which curl when they fall will do, while those which lie flat will not. Leaves may be collected in baskets or piled in a corner of the yard until needed in mid-December or later if a hard freeze has not occurred by that time. Then they are spread in place and a few evergreen boughs, perhaps the lopped-off Christmas tree branches, are placed on top to hold them in place.

Salt hay is another fine well-aerated mulching material. It can be purchased by the bale and used for more than one winter although between seasons it must be stored where it is not a fire hazard. And finally if the compost pit contains enough partially rotted year-old leaves, a two-inch layer of these will suffice for a winter blanket and the finer part of them will be excellent for working into the soil in spring.

With plants which maintain green tops like the foxglove and hollyhock, coverings are drawn under not over the tops. For these and woolly-leaved subjects like the mulleins, and some gardeners say delphiniums too, a layer of stone is excellent. De Petris chrysanthemums with their green crowns require no covering whatever, while peonies and iris, too, are better uncovered except their first year after planting. All young plants, not far beyond the seedling stage, are mulched earlier than established perennials. This is to conserve autumn warmth and so prolong their growing stage. Early November is usually not too soon to protect them.

In spring the greater part of the mulch is removed just as the forsythias bloom while the final amount is lifted as the buds appear on the maple trees. No exact dates can be set since the end of winter differs not only with localities but with the different years. Late in March is the time most of us have a winter-underwear feeling about mulches. Then it is time to poke underneath leaves or hay and see what goes on. Very likely coverings can be loosened a little to aerate the awakening plants. Mulches left too long in place force abnormal growth but if spring fever gets the gardener's ambition in operation too early, she may invite a touch of frostbite for her perennials by removing winter protection while spring is still much too far behind.

❧ ❧

CHAPTER IV

SUPPORTS FOR GIANTS AND SPREADERS

GOOD looks in a garden depend to a great extent on tidiness. This is particularly true of small plots. In these no amount of handsome individual flowers will give a good effect if scattered about are supine plants which should be perpendicular rather than prone.

To maintain uprightness through the border I subscribe definitely to a far-sighted program. This means the occasional use only of certain loose-growing subjects like the lovely *Salvia azurea* which invariably needs special attention. Penstemons, bergamot and most physostegias are other rampant flounderers. Before banishing, however, it is wise to consider whether the inertness of a plant is an inherent characteristic, as it certainly is of these, or a weak condition due to a soil lack which should be remedied at the source with applications of phosphorus in the form of bone meal in the fall and superphosphate in the spring.

Many plants despite soil, however, require support against wind and summer rain. This need brings the forehanded gardener at spring ordering time to a most fascinating collection of gadgetry. When I bring my box out on Stake Day I find I have quite a variety. These have been acquired over a period of years according to the needs of individual plant groups as I became aware of them.

WHO GETS SATISFACTION FROM SUCH STAKING!
NOT THE PLANT.

The newer supports are quite different from the stout broom or mop handles which once sufficed. When these were plunged into the center of recalcitrant growers and the foliage drawn up and bunched together with heavy white cord, it is doubtful who got any satisfaction from the process. Certainly not the plants. They seemed in their unnatural state to be suffering continuous indignity, while the beauty-loving gardener knew something was wrong, even if no other method of dealing with floppy plants occurred to her.

Today we respect the natural tendencies of growth.

When the garden abounds in platycodon, veronica, coreopsis, gaillardia, oriental poppies and achillea, twiggy growth is early set among them so that, as the plants develop, they arrange themselves naturally over their supports and these are eventually hidden. You can have a convenient source of just the right kind of twiggy branches if you will plant, for the purpose, in some out-of-the-way corner, a couple of bushes of California privet and allow them to grow unpruned.

When twigs do not suffice, you must buy various plant supports and some "ties" of one kind or another too. Once it seemed to me that staking and tying involved so many operations at once that I needed an extra hand. All this is now simplified.

For single-stemmed plants I use assorted lengths of bamboo and wire, not held in place by string or tape but by a handy little wire clip called a Plant Tie, or by a flexible wire tape or 'Twistem designed on the pipe-cleaner plan. Both of these are as easy to fasten securely as a bobby pin and they provide enough "give" to prevent breaking.

Natural color bamboo is less expensive than that dyed green, but the green ones are worth the difference because they show less. Galvanized iron wire one-eighth inch in diameter and in two to six-foot lengths I like even better, because it is narrow yet very strong. When there are many separate stems as in mature meadowrue or delphinium, I clip a separate wire support to each. This is a beautifully neat and strong arrangement.

For such plants I like, too, when I can obtain it, a

special Bloom Support made with eight-inch adjustable arms. Any number of arms can be clipped to the single wire upright which is inserted into the side or center of the clump, not too deeply, of course, if the variety is shallow-rooting. Then the various stems, as many as look well, are drawn toward the eight-inch radius and firmly held there by a bent groove in the adjustable arm. I specially like these supports for the large flowering chrysanthemums which have been disbudded in the interest of specimen blooms.

For bunchier plants, like my blue flax, pyrethrums, and oriental poppies, I prefer the Timesaver Plant Support equipped with a strong, green, silken cord clipped to the upright wire support. This is easily drawn around the stems about halfway up the plant and fastened without tying to a notch made for it. On the same principle is an adjustable wire ring which can be slid up a stout wooden stake as the spreading plant grows. But I can't abide this kind. It's such a clumsy, stalwart object that even a few placed with every effort at concealment stuck out in my garden as conspicuously as a straw hat before June.

For peonies, and the more rampant chrysanthemums, I like the double ring Model Peony Trellis of tripod type. Some gardeners use this also for large delphinium and oriental poppy clumps. Thrust among the plants early, it it soon covered by new growth. Two kinds of double ring supports have been available, one with the top ring adjustable. I prefer the type with both rings stationary because it wears better. Mine now have eight years of double duty to their credit. In April they are thrust deeply around each clump of peonies. In late June, they are transferred for the summer to those chrysanthemums destined for prolific autumn display. With either full grown plant they are blessedly invisible.

And that is the aim of proper plant supporting—invisibility. If visitors to the garden ever remark, "What interesting supports you are using," or, "How carefully you stake your plants," I know that that season I have done but an inept job.

CHAPTER V

GUIDES TO GARDEN HEALTH

SUCCESSFUL coping with pest and disease seems to be a necessary though completely unappealing aspect of gardening. But you can mitigate the pain considerably, I have discovered, by eliminating all but the sturdier plant varieties and also by careful garden sanitation. This means keeping a clean garden, burning disease-ridden stalks and yellowing leaves, and not planting so thickly that you check a free circulation of cleansing air.

Even the not-too-serious among us, however, have some pet perennials on which we are willing to lavish a certain amount of extra effort, providing, of course, there are rewards. With these plants in mind, I schedule the first and fifteenth of each month from April to September as my doctoring days. Perennials I can not keep in satisfactory condition on such a schedule I usually replace since spending the summer in the role of bug detector will never be my idea of a good time, no matter how handsome the garden grows.

To make even my simple program effective, however, some knowledge of what is being controlled or fought is essential. Shadow boxing in a garden never produces healthy results. For example, attacking a sucking insect with arsenate of lead, which is a stomach poison for chewers, is only a waste of time. It achieves nothing but frustration. Which brings me to the time-honored and classic division of insect pests—the suckers and the chewers, each of which is vulnerable to attack, but in a different way.

Sucking insects weaken or destroy by piercing plant tissues with their beaks and drawing from them the vital juices. General debility and loss of color follow an attack. The most common insect in this class is the APHID, black groups of which are all too familiar on the succulent young shoots of chrysanthemums, while lighter ones cluster on the underside of columbine foliage. Any time after growth commences in spring, aphids—black, green, white or red—may make an appearance. Their doom is known as the "contact insecticide" because it kills by covering the pest and smothering it through the stoppage of its breathing pores.

There are numerous good contact insecticides. Basically they are now made of nicotine, rotenone, pyrethrum or some combination of these, but what amazing panaceas the future will offer is anybody's guess. Rotenone and pyrethrum have the advantage of being absolutely nonpoisonous to humans and they do not discolor. Select any one of the good standard products and use it every fortnight on plants likely to be bothered.

This is a preventive measure for such perennials as chrysanthemums. Should an aphid attack outwit you, be more drastic. Dust or spray for three successive days in order to catch by the third day any nymphs or eggs which may have hatched since your first onslaught. Thorough coverage on upper and *under* leaf surfaces is essential, since the contact insecticide kills only what it strikes.

The RED SPIDER and other mites are very inclined to arrive with their families in the humid heat of the summer just when control measures are the last thing you feel like attempting. Make a mighty effort on the firsts and fifteenths, however, for you can't wait to see this pest which is invisible to the naked eye. Phlox, hollyhocks and the hardy evergreen candytuft or iberis are favorite abodes which benefit by preventive coverage.

Forceful hose sprays aimed from beneath the plant will break the red spider webs and do a lot toward eradication. Be sure to practice this control early in the day. (Foliage which is sprinkled late in the afternoon of a muggy week is a prey to other troubles.) Better still, haul out your contact killer. Or you can do away with the red spider when you don't feel like heaving a sprayer or duster around in the heat, by spreading fine dusting sulphur with a spoon under each vulnerable plant so as to cover the soil lightly. Scattered on a very hot day, it will act as a deadly fumigant, gassing the spiders right into eternity.

The attack of the chewing insects is not so subtle. They move forth and chew until they skeletonize. Stomach poisons consumed as they devour foliage are their doom. The best known horror among chewers is the JAPANESE BEETLE. When plants like hollyhocks need protection, spray with one of the beetle preparations at emerging time (June 20 in Philadelphia and 30 in New York) and again on August 1 or 10. Or omit hollyhocks for a few years. Japanese beetles eventually leave a locality, you know. I never have more than one or two a season here now but time was—but over that era of my gardening, let me draw a veil.

BORERS OR CATERPILLARS which work inside stems are likewise chewers and very hard to deal with. Sometimes they can be caught working and destroyed on the spot. Dusting their favorite, the bearded iris, in May with a pyrethrum or rotenone and sulphur preparation helps. (See page 76.)

Occasionally trouble originates in the soil, as when CUTWORMS attack the columbines or various seedlings just after you have proudly set them out. There are several standard products to take care of them. Or you can insert into the soil a stiff paper collar around each plant. And if you scatter shingles about you will find under them in the morning cutworms which you can then promptly dispatch.

ANTS may cause trouble, not on peony buds, from which they disappear when the flower opens, but in flower beds where their busy hills are objectionable. Enlarge nest holes with a skewer and pour carbon bisulphide, a full tablespoonful, into each. Then plug up with mud. (Beware of smoking while engaged in this business or it may not be the ant which suffers annihilation.) You might also try ant traps or one of the labeled ant destroyers, but the carbon bisulphide has done best by me and for moles as well as ants.

It would be pleasant if at this point I could end my homily of sorrow with the assurance that not all gardens get all the pests, nor even some of them, every year. Which is, indeed, a comforting as well as a true thought. I must add, however, that there are fungous troubles, diseases, which must also be dealt with. Three kinds are most common—mildew, leaf blights of many kinds and rusts.

Mildew, which covers with a white powdery coating plants of peony, phlox, chrysanthemum and delphinium when July and August days are damp and muggy, may be cleaned up by dusting with finely divided sulphur at any time trouble appears. Crowded, damp or sunless plantings, where the atmosphere is close, are the most prone to attack, or those gardens which are persistently sprinkled at dusk so that foliage goes into the night wet.

Among leaf blights, black spot on delphiniums, which mars, curls and disfigures foliage, is common. Sulphur will prevent it. Peonies on which buds blacken and fail to open are affected by a fungus known as botrytis blight. Bordeaux mixture has long been the standard control. I dust it on peonies when they are wet with dew from the time the spring points emerge until the foliage is about one foot high. For the rust of hollyhock a sulphur dust is adequate.

Two pieces of equipment are necessary for garden doctoring: a duster and a sprayer, small or large according to the number of plants to be tended. And in my opinion you will be wise to select dusts and to use a duster in preference to a sprayer any time you can. It seems to me far simpler to transfer a dry material from package to dust gun than to go through the measuring and diluting process for sprays and then afterwards to wash and dry your sprayer.

The Spraying School maintains, however, that you get a more thorough coverage with a spray and also that it sticks longer, especially if in mixing insecticides or fungicides you have added some good prepared spreader or just common soap flakes of your own concocting. Even so, I dust when plants are wet and if occasionally I think the phlox needs an extra going over on an off-schedule day, I find it no trouble at all to pick up my duster, which I keep filled with a sulphur or rotenone preparation, and give the plants a few clouds of protective film.

Now if you are a beginning gardener, don't be appalled by the pages devoted to insecticides and fungicides in your favorite catalogue and this first year don't try to digest a book which treats the entire horrid subject. Instead obtain early in the season five pounds or so, depending on your garden size, of one of the all-purpose dusts. These are combinations of nicotine or pyrethrum, rotenone and sulphur. A simple control program consists in applying either of these or something similar twice a month on all your perennials. Begin in mid-April and end the business in mid-September, about ten applications in all.

Keep in mind that your purpose is to prevent, rather than to control. Then be faithful about the job. You will be surprised what a small part of a morning hour this sensible routine will require and how healthy your borders will stay. As you become more experienced you can be less wasteful of materials, and this is a somewhat wasteful plan, since to hit a chewer you are also using a contact material for suckers as well as applying sulphur to plants not perhaps requiring blight protection. Later you can learn to select separate controls as you discover what things bother what plants and when is the best time to apply preventive measures.

Sometimes Forget the Dust Gun
and Employ the Fan.

You can save yourself a lot of trouble too by being sensible in your choice of plant material. If you find delphiniums are one long headache or peonies blight more than they bloom and you are tired to death of their temperamental demands, for heaven's sake, throw them out. Life is too short to let gardening be more chore than fun. Emphasize more robust material so you can have a fan in your hand part of the summer instead of a duster or spray gun.

Having thus handed over to you the fruits of my sometimes bitter experience, I won't here name the plants nothing will ever again induce me to try. But I will suggest that you consider this list of kinds which for me have been singularly free from the exigencies of fate. Fill your garden with the likes of these if healthful abundance is for you an important aspect of your garden.

Plants That Help Themselves

Astilbe (Spiraea)
Baptisia (False Indigo)
Chrysanthemum maximum (Shasta Daisy)
Convallaria (Lily-of-the-Valley)
Coreopsis
Delphinium (only the Chinese type)
Dianthus (Pinks)
Dicentra (Bleedingheart)
Dictamnus (Gas Plant)
Doronicum (Leopardbane)
Eupatorium
Funkia or *Hosta* (August Lilies and their relatives)
Gaillardia (Blanket Flower)
Gypsophila (Babysbreath)
Helenium (Helen's Flower)
Heliopsis (Orange Sunflower)
Helleborus niger (Christmas Rose)
Hemerocallis (Daylily)
Heuchera (Coralbell)
Iris sibirica (Siberian Iris)
Linum (Flax)
Monarda (Beebalm)

Papaver orientale (Oriental Poppy)
Phlox subulata
Physostegia (False Dragonhead)
Polemonium reptans (Jacob's Ladder)
Primula (Primrose)
Pyrethrum
Salvia azurea
Thalictrum (Meadowrue)
Thermopsis
Veronica
Viola (Violet)

All of the self-help plants are not distinguished or even refined growers but they are sturdy. Many, however, like the bleedinghearts, are the loveliest possible garden flowers while such perennials as baptisia, gas plant and hosta have an enduringly fine plant form with consistent attractiveness from spring to fall. Peonies, hybrid delphinium, bearded iris and phlox are not included although we consider these first when we plan a border. For reasons which you may happily never discover for yourself, I omit them from this list of essentially reliable plants.

Control Chart

(See Separate Chapters for Gruesome Details!)

PLANT AND AILMENT	CAUSE	CONTROL
Althaea rosea (Hollyhock)		
Poor foliage rusty beneath or yellow webbed	Rust or red spider	Dust with sulphur or rotenone.
Foliage with holes	Japanese beetles	Spray with a Japanese beetle repellent. Omit hollyhocks in areas of severe beetle infestation.

Plant and Ailment	Cause	Control
Anemone japonica		
Chewed look to foliage and flowers	Long, dark or striped beetles	Catch what you can. Dust with pyrethrum or rotenone.
Aquilegia (Columbine)		
Light labyrinthian markings on foliage	Leaf miner	Remove infected leaves. Dust from June on with nicotine or rotenone.
Pale insect clusters on underside of leaves	Aphids	Same dust directed from beneath plant.
Chrysanthemum		
Lower leaves turn dry and brown	A weather factor or a nematode attack	Keep well watered in dry spells. Remove badly affected plants. Dust others regularly with nicotine or rotenone.
Leaf tips curling and covered with black insects	Aphids	Same dust control.
Brown spots on foliage	Leaf blight	Dust with sulphur.
White coating	Mildew	Dust with sulphur.
Delphinium		
Distorted leaf and stem growth and blackened flower stalks	Cyclamen mite	Destroy the worst plants. Dust others regularly and before trouble with rotenone or sulphur.
Leaves curl down	Red lice on underside	Dust with nicotine or rotenone.
Blackening and rotting of whole plant	Crown rot	Remove worst plants. Maintain a sulphur dust on others.
Dark spotting of leaves	Black spot	Carefully pick off and burn affected foliage. Dust with sulphur.
White coating of leaves from midsummer on	Mildew	Sulphur dust. (All-purpose rose dust or spray, such as Triogen, a good routine for delphinium if there are a number of plants.)

Plant and Ailment	Cause	Control
Iris		
Pierced ragged spots on foliage, water-soaked look	Borer, a pale caterpillar working between leaves in spring and then down into rhizome. Eggs winter in old leaves and debris	Sanitation. Remove and burn old foliage early in spring. Dust the new in May with pyrethrum or rotenone and sulphur. Remove observed borers by piercing leaf with knife tip or sever leaves below point of attack.
Leaves rotting at ground line. Foul odor when pulled off	Bacterial root rot, caused by winter injury or tunneling borers	Clean up borers. Where much damage, lift roots, cut out decay, dust with sulphur, dry in sun and replant. Or try early spring spraying several times at ground line with bordeaux mixture.
Paeonia		
Grayish mold at base, toppling over young stems or just bud blasting while buds are small	Botrytis blight	Sanitation is first control. Cut off affected buds and stems and burn. Cut off open flowers, before they shatter, and burn. In fall cut off all foliage to ground and burn.
		Dust with bordeaux mixture in spring as soon as shoots appear. Repeat until foliage is twelve inches high.
Insects crawling on partly opened buds	Ants	No control, no damage being done.
Phlox		
Browning of lower foliage	Probably drought	Water *deeply* in dry spells.
Moldy white appearance of leaves	Mildew	Dust regularly with sulphur.
Yellowing of leaves	Red spider	Good sulphur coverage also checks this.

❧ ❧

CHAPTER VI

MEANS OF MULTIPLICATION

WHEN the plan for your perennial garden has reached the completed drawn-to-scale on-paper stage, where will you find your plants? At the risk of sounding cynical I advise you to depend very little on the bounty of friends and neighbors. Don't mind, indeed, looking the gift horse very searchingly in the mouth since all too often the given plant turns out to be magenta phlox, orange daylily, fried-egg iris or the all-encompassing golden glow. Only rarely is it a fine strain of columbine seedlings or divisions from a pale and scented hemerocallis. As a particular gardener, even if a new one, you want only choice perennials and of these no one ever seems to have many to give away.

Next about buying. If a local nursery can supply you with well-developed clumps, neither barely started seedlings nor minute divisions, make your selections there. Then new plants will not have to suffer the rigors of travel. And when you buy, be certain you are getting the varieties you desire. Nothing so upsets a well-laid scheme as the planting of the loud yellow basket-of-gold, *Alyssum saxatile compactum* when it was the lemon yellow *A. saxatile citrinum* you ordered, or the placing of a salmon pink phlox where you wanted a delicate rose variety.

At the start, consider well worth obtaining by purchase fine varieties of iris, hybrid delphinium, peony, chrysanthemum, hardy aster, oriental poppy, helenium, babysbreath, bleedingheart, gas plant, baptisia, anemone, aconite, daylily, hardy candytuft, mertensia and hellebore.

You do not, however, need quantities of these. Three or more, depending on space, will suffice of the delphinium, iris, anemone, gas plant, mertensia and aconite. But one each is enough of the named varieties of chrysanthemum, aster, most daisies and babysbreath since all of these soon lend themselves to simple means of home propagation. And, of course, with the more expensive kinds of peony and oriental poppy one each is plenty unless you are familiar with the variety.

Until I learned the danger of blind ordering, I sometimes used to be inundated with twelve plants of something rampant like helenium when with a little patience I could have had my twelve by the second year from one bought plant. Once I purchased nine *Artemisia lactiflora*, "Hawthorne-scented, five feet, exquisite combined with buddleia and hardy asters" and found myself in possession of an enormous crop of something very near a weed. I do not mean, of course, for you to be a one-of-each buyer or planter. Catalogues sensibly encourage selection by threes. From an economical and practical point of view, however, your larger purchases should be of plants hard to propagate at home such as delphinium in some places, or slow like the peony or gas plant or scarce like hellebores.

Meanwhile purchased stock can be increased in three ways—by division, by stem cuttings or by root cuttings.

After heleniums, shasta daisies and most chrysanthemums have grown in your garden for only a year you can lift the plants with a spading fork, in spring, and carefully pull, pry, or cut them into a number of divisions. These set out separately will by summer or fall give you new plants of a size equal to the parents. Phlox, iris and columbine can be divided by the third year.

When you lift some plants a hard woody center will appear. Discard this, resetting only the younger sections. But don't make the divisions too small or the next year your garden will have a very sparse and meager look indeed. Experience will reveal each plant's rate of development. You will discover that a well-grown phlox can usually be separated into thirds while every small piece of rooted chrysanthemum has the capacity for equaling its mature parent within the one growing season.

And you will find that spring- and summer-flowering plants like iris, phlox, columbine and primrose are best divided after a rain in late August or September. Deal with them as soon as the heat has sufficiently waned for you to attack the business cheerfully but while at least a month or more of growing weather continues before frost. This allows divided plants to anchor themselves in their new locations. Plan spring division for chrysanthemums, hardy asters, aconites and other fall-flowering plants. Some perennials like the peony, gypsophila, bleedingheart, lupine, gas plant, anemone and Christmas rose you will not disturb for years and years since these flourish only after they have been thoroughly acclimated to your garden.

Another method of increase is by cuttings—stem or root. When the second growth of rockcress, hardy candytuft, phlox or pinks is well advanced, just go through the plantings with a razor blade. Exactly beneath the point where a leaf emerges, cut the stems off. Leave several eyes or points of growth, of course, below the cut so that the older plant can sprout again. This treatment does not harm developed perennials. It only makes them thick and branching.

Next, from the cut sections you have taken, remove the lower leaves and any incipient flowers at the top. Then insert the bare stems an inch or so of their approximately three-inch lengths in a box of moist sand set in the shade or in a shaded cold frame. In this way you can quickly and easily obtain a large crop of one variety. I have had Lingard phlox root in less than three weeks in August and with almost no attention from me. If you want to obtain economically an edging of one kind, like hardy candytuft, for instance, try this method of increase after your three or more purchased plants are established.

The root cutting is a good way to extend your stock of bleedinghearts, phlox, sea lavender, babysbreath, anemone and oriental poppy. In late August or September lift the plant you wish to propagate and select roots of approximately lead pencil size. Cut these into three-inch pieces and lay the sections horizontally in rows in a cold frame. Space them about three inches apart and firm over them a one to two-inch layer of sand or sand and peat moss mixed. Leave the frame open until after freezing weather. Then close and shade it until warm middays occur in February. Begin to ventilate for progressively longer periods as the spring season advances. Water from April on as the soil requires it. By May you will have a fine lusty crop of complete plants to move to permanent quarters.

Some plants grow so readily from seed it is really extravagant to obtain them any other way. This is true of all the biennials like the campanulas and foxgloves and also of many perennials. Peonies, iris, phlox, and daylily are not propagated from seed, however, since these are hybrids and do not "come true," meaning they do not faithfully duplicate their parents.

Sow seeds of the various biennials and perennials you are propagating at approximately the same time they would sow themselves, if nature were permitted her own course. Make exceptions only of pansies, which develop more satisfactorily if sowing is delayed until the midsummer heat is past, of September Jewel chrysanthemums, which behave practically like annuals, and of delphinium. Of this you want fresh seed and unless you are using your own, it cannot be purchased before late July. As for the rest, sow the spring-flowering arabis, alyssum, columbine, iberis and primrose preferably in May and June; the early summer lupines, foxgloves, coralbells, campanulas, meadowrue, thermopsis and pyrethrum before the end of July; and the aconite, gaillardia, platycodon, salvia, scabiosa, shasta daisy, stokesia and other summer- and fall-blooming perennials between mid-July and mid-August.

Make your sowings either in a cold frame or in the open near a hedge or wall. Keep in mind that your success depends on a constant supply of moisture, protection from wind and strong sunshine and a loose soil which will neither bake out nor drain rapidly. Prepare the top inch of soil with particular care. Finely pulverized humus or compost will improve texture with sand liberally added if the soil is heavy.

Sow the seeds thinly and evenly and press them lightly into the soil. Then water gently. I use the house plant syringe or my quart can sprayer for this purpose. Finally cover with a thin layer of soil and never for a minute thereafter neglect that need for even moisture. Sowings are easily protected from glare and drying wind by a lath shade.

Meanwhile prepare a second bed or another cold frame section to receive the seedlings as soon as they are of a size to handle conveniently. Use plenty of humus in this second bed but no chemical fertilizers. Space the plants according to their natures from three inches for iberis to nine inches for foxgloves. Provide protection from the sun for the first week after transplanting and cultivate carefully by hand. Many perennials, of course, may be propagated in several ways depending on your preference and convenience.

Of course, you must have a cold frame. Even if your garden is small, gardening without one is like cooking without electric appliances. You can do it, but it's more work and less fun. In its basic form a cold frame is simply a box without top and bottom. For bottom it has the soil; for top, a piece of glass. In a sunny spot this wooden frame is inserted into the ground so that the front rests about ten inches above soil level and the rear twenty. Thus a sloping surface is provided to catch sunshine. For cold protection the box is banked with several inches of soil on the outside and in extreme weather burlap bags or a piece of blanket or carpet is thrown over the glass at night to keep in the warmth the sun afforded during the day.

My first cold frame was simply a wooden grocery box inserted into the soil near the kitchen door where the sun could warm it quickly and I could examine it constantly. For in my early days of gardening I was certainly one to watch the pot until I wonder it ever boiled.

Anyway it was amazing the crops I grew there using a cheap adjustable window screen as a sun shade in the heat. Late in March I'd start a crop of Chinese larkspur along with one of the slow annuals like the petunias. When these were moved in May, I put in cuttings of Miss Lingard phlox followed by a sowing of Mrs. Scott Elliott columbines which remained until the next spring. Thus that little makeshift structure was put to use every month of the year.

Today I work on a little larger scale. I have a triple cold frame now (see Portfolio) its tops made from casements taken from the children's torn-down playhouse and its sides from creosoted floor boards from the same source. My husband made it one Armistice Day and the only new materials he used were two by four posts cut into lengths to form strong corners. Later he obtained a bundle of lath from which he made the slatted covers which give such excellent protection to summer sowings. The end sections of this frame measure eighteen by thirty-six inches; the middle is only ten inches wide.

I have never owned a so-called Regulation Cold Frame made of three by six standard sash. I hope I never shall. These are ungainly for a woman to handle and also not nearly so convenient as several small frames in which different length operations can be carried on at the same time.

Besides a spot for plant propagation frames also offer safe winter quarters for tender plants like spoon chrysanthemums or gerberas which are moved there after they stop flowering. Cuttings and seedlings still too small for outside wintering can likewise be stored there during the cold months. And I like an extra one too for a permanent crop. I particularly enjoy a small duplex built in a sun-drenched corner by the study steps. Here I have a planting of *Iris stylosa* and sweet violets—very nice for midwinter and early spring picking.

Without a cold frame you can still raise many perennials from seed or cutting. A somewhat raised bed in a light but not sunny, protected spot outdoors near the hose will do. Or a box of well-prepared soil makes a nice nursery. After sowing cover with a piece of burlap to keep the soil from drying out. Water right through this until germination occurs. But at the sign of the first green shoot, whisk away the burlap, for plants have been known to get their young necks broken if they poked them through burlap weave. You cannot regulate conditions so well in the open and, of course, you cannot sow early nor protect plants late.

So do have a cold frame, even a makeshift one like my own early love.

CHAPTER VII

IMPORTANT PERENNIALS FOR SPRING

1. Iris, Indispensable and Irresistible

IN THE temperate zone, the iris, or fleur-de-lis, Ruskin's flower of chivalry, "with a sword for its leaf and a lily for its heart," is a cherished perennial. Alone in spacious hobby gardens it makes a magnificent spring and early summer picture with long drifts of translucent white passing into cream and yellow, and pink, lavender, purple and red terminating in masses of seashell and sunset blends. Indeed, iris is so dear to most of us that even when our space is limited we designate that area of the border behind edging plants and early bulbs as The Iris Strip. Here we set out a colorful array of intermediate and tall bearded varieties for May and June and perhaps autumn bloom and are pleased to give them foreground placement because their foliage has such fine enduring quality.

Actually, however, May is much too late for me to start my iris story. I want to commence in December with the species *Iris stylosa* or *unguicularis* which, established in one section of a cold frame, produces early in winter after it has been lightly touched by frost exquisite flowers "of real sky blue—not the deep blue of summer, but the brilliant paler blue of a frosty January." *Stylosa* may not flower the first season it is set out but it produces winter bouquets the second or third as it gets to feeling at home in the coarse sandy or gravelly soil provided. Of course it cannot conveniently be moved in and out of the cold frame but must occupy a section permanently.

Stylosa is followed in April by a bright amethyst patch of that crested little species, *Iris cristata.* Under the apple tree with White Lady narcissus this little charmer is one of the first delights of my spring garden. A moist soil, rich in humus and a lightly shaded location constitute its happy life. Perhaps in your rock garden you too can find just the spot for it.

I must also have a few plants of the roof iris (*I. tectorum*) which in China blooms purple and white on thatched roofs like flowers on a lady's hat. These twelve-inch plants, in the white variety, *alba,* are pleasing when alternately grouped with lavender *Phlox divaricata.* The blue one is attractive with early yellow tulips. Shade and soil from the compost pit also delight *tectorum.*

In many gardens the dwarf iris, *I. pumila,* now begins to flower, but not in mine. This is an iris I definitely cannot abide. It looks all wrong to me, those big blooms and those little plants, ugly, somehow, the way dwarfs are ugly and physically not well composed. No, indeed, no *Iris pumila* for me, let the catalogue color plates bleat as they will.

But the tall and dignified Siberians, how I treasure these. If you have known only the familiar bearded iris, do now make the acquaintance of this beardless type which flowers from about mid-May to mid-June. It develops strong clumps three to four feet tall with slender, grassy foliage and a quantity of individual stems each carrying a half dozen or so delicate white, lavender or violet blooms which usually appear just before the tall bearded varieties.

Because these Siberians present the dual blessing of flower quality and extreme ease of culture they are just the plants for every one of you whose time is at a premium. I have grown the older varieties like Perry's Blue and Snow Queen for years and years and years, in a richly prepared border as well as in the less mellow shrubbery line where they also provided quantities of bouquets. Although there was, of course, a difference in flower quality, both plantings required little beyond a few deep soakings prior to blooming, if the season was dry, the clipping off of faded flower stems and the division of roots once in four years. Bone meal and pulverized manure are good soil conditioners for these completely pest- and disease-free perennials. And after the first winter you do not even have to bother with a cold weather covering.

Their garden uses are, indeed, multiple. When you plant Siberians, space several single divisions three to four inches apart to form a clump. Even one of each color will afford quantities of cut flowers. You can naturalize Perry's Blue delightfully or fit Red Emperor or the mauve Helen Astor into the landscape design as a facing-down plant for shrubs or along a low porch to conceal foundations.

In the border, varieties like Snow Crest or Martha le Grand form strong, pleasing white accents. Siberians look well, too, in separate beds where after flowering their foliage continues excellently green. Or they may be combined with other perennials. The clear blue Gatineau is handsome with such an early daylily as Apricot while the dark, pansy-purple Caesar's Brother or bright blue Mountain Lake is an ideal companion for the sulphur white peony Duchesse de Nemours.

At about the same time as the Siberians, or sometimes a little before them, the early bearded varieties of iris begin to bloom. Among these do consider the intermediates which I find so attractive to flank the taller kinds in the border. Of sturdy constitution, they grow from sixteen to twenty-eight inches tall and are, indeed, intermediate in size of flower and height. Some kinds, like Autumn Frost and Autumn Haze, tend to repeat their pleasing performance in the fall. A few, like Autumn Queen, often flower intermittently through the summer. But do not count on this later blooming as a certainty although it does sometimes occur on varieties sold as fall-flowering. It is in May that you will find such intermediates as the white Cosette, golden Crysora, yellow Nymph and Andalusian Blue ideal and dependable companions for tulips or even substitutes for them—just the perennial, in fact, to fill in a possible lull following narcissus.

The taller bearded iris have in recent years undergone a transformation which makes the varieties of today a far and joyful cry from the muddy purples and blurred yellows of the plants we knew in childhood as flags. Selecting a limited group, however, is complicated business. For varieties now number thousands with a flowering period from mid-May far into June and heights varying from thirty to fifty inches.

But you must be self-controlled with iris or your garden becomes a melée. Certainly in the mixed border repeated groups of just a few varieties give a far lovelier effect than a confusion of numerous kinds, fine as each may be. And I grow only the "selfs" or varieties of one color. I think bicolors, blends and even the "stitched" plicatas incline to spotty effects and my cut-flower arrangements are never sufficiently subtle for me to struggle with their dual shadings.

When I plant bearded iris in the border I arrange it in long rectangles or ovals, with specimen plants of hemerocallis to interrupt and separate the iris colonies. This gives a pleasant effect in bloom and later the whole line remains unfalteringly green. Through the summer then I occasionally trim back the daylilies to keep them from shading the iris.

If your garden is quite small, three to five plants are enough for each colony. Where space permits, use larger groups of one kind. Seek attractive companions among daylilies, oriental poppies, columbines and peonies and for minor harmonies use pinks, coralbells and flax. Try the white iris Gudrun and the yellow Eclador with the silvery pink and fragrant peony Mons. Jules Elie or place together the dwarf iris Snowdrop, the taller Shining Sun and the white peony Le Cygne. With a deep variety like iris Red Douglas, use blue lupines and white meadowrue.

Perhaps you will prefer tall bearded iris separately in bold clumps of one color. In the intersection of garden paths five to seven plants of one of the blends like Copper Lustre would be handsome or a flight of steps might be graced by the Carrara whiteness of Venus de Milo. Red Velvet or any other dark kind looks well along a white fence while the very tall *pallida dalmatica*, Princess Beatrice, requires a background of evergreens or house wall.

If you have a rather small layout but wish to feature iris, arrange it so as to simulate depth. I once saw in an almost square plot, with a paved circular center, iris set in skillful gradations in deep triangular corner beds to give perspective. The whites and yellows were planted in the foreground. These have, of course, the strongest visual value. The blues and pinks were behind them with the deeper violets like Blue Velvet giving an effect of distance in the background. Extremely dark or "black" varieties were wisely omitted. These require lighter varieties among them to set them off and even then may not be so telling as the translucent blues or glowing yellows.

These bearded iris have two definite requirements—drainage and plenty of sunshine. They are a joy even to us who suffer with a cement-mix soil and they seem to thrive in alkaline, neutral or slightly acid loam of average fertility. For extra food, use a light sprinkling of bone meal in fall and of pulverized sheep manure or a balanced fertilizer in spring. Be sure to plant the rhizomes with the top of the fleshy roots but half an inch or so under the surface of the soil. Here they can bask in the sun. If set deeper they will either refuse to bloom, die of discouragement or energetically work their way up to their favorite position.

And don't attempt to cultivate iris in the usual way. Roots lie too near the surface for safe hoeing. Weed the plants by hand instead. And clean them up in spring as early and as thoroughly as possible. Then remove all old leaves and debris to prevent attacks of the now too familiar iris borer which winters over in eggs deposited by a moth the previous fall. I find this particularly annoying because for so many years I have comfortably assumed that iris was an absolutely pest-free and unparticular perennial. Now I must regularly contend with the borer which first punctures foliage, then waxing fat and happy with the iris as a feeding ground, slowly works its way down into the rhizome. Decay and iris rot follow its abode although rot may occur from other causes as well, winter injury being one.

If your plants have revealed zigzag edges and lines of slime, if flower stalks have toppled over and there have been many yellow leaves and if on pulling these out, you have easily yanked out pieces of decayed evil-smelling rhizome as well, you know to your sorrow just what I mean. Now besides Dutch-housekeeping sanitary measures this is what you can do. Early in May, apply a protective film of pyrethrum or rotenone and sulphur to the dewy foliage. Dust a second time if rain washes away the coating before the flower buds show color. And if you see a punctured leaf and signs of borer activity, cut the foliage off below the point of attack and burn it. Or try to slay the invader by squeezing the leaves between two fingers—an extremely effective if unpleasant procedure.

Sometimes without the borer, leaf tips wither and brown and appear water-soaked at the base. When rhizome rot is thus in evidence, lift the plants and cut out any soft portions with a sharp knife. Then dust the cuts with powdered sulphur and for a few days let the rhizome lie exposed to the sun. When you see that the decay has been arrested, replant the rhizomes in a new location if possible or in fresh soil in their former place.

The best time for such repair work and for the separating of overthick bearded iris is between July and September. Wait, however, until in their third or fourth year plants are falling off in quality of bloom before you lift healthy clumps. Then trim the fan tops halfway back, pull the plants apart and reset small divisions shallowly and at twelve-inch distances. Face all the rhizomes the same way and plant in rows, not circles around a hole, since this center space never fills in properly.

The first winter after planting mulch lightly but afterwards omit this protection unless you live in a subzero section. In spring, however, go over the plantings early to press back into the soil any frost-heaved plants. Although established iris is quite drought tolerant, newly set plantings need extra water if a dry spell follows their transplanting. Sometimes, too, brown leaf tips on older plants in times of drought indicate the need for a thorough soaking. Finally, make it a routine matter to relieve plants promptly of the stems of faded flowers at the ground line. This helps to let in to each clump more health-giving sun and air.

From mid-June until mid-July after the pageantry of the tall bearded iris has subsided a completely different type, *Iris kaempferi*, or Japanese iris, now called oriental, comes into beauty. Blooming for the most part after the first delphiniums and before summer phlox, the large flowers—six to ten inches across—bring strong color to the border while for cutting they are unbelievably beautiful. Especially to those who are adept at arrangements in the oriental manner is the *kaempferi* iris challenging material.

Plants vary in height from thirty to fifty inches, a matter more of moisture and fertility than of variety, although Gold Bound is always shorter. The singles show three large and three small petals. Then there are doubles and triples with six or more petals or petal-like forms. Colors run from luscious deep, deep purple through burgundy and pink shades to soft blues and whites with striking yellow markings. Indeed, I cannot recall seeing any variety I could dislike.

Success with this *Iris kaempferi* is dependent on three factors—a well-drained site, a soil rich in organic matter, and above all, and this is the real key to success, abundant moisture, especially during the growing season.

Many gardeners would also advise acidity declaring that flowering noticeably improved after aluminum sulphate, sulphur, or acid peat moss was liberally worked into the soil around their plants. If you have a pool or stream, by all means plant oriental iris beside it. There reflection will make its exceptional beauty doubly enchanting and plenty of water keeps it culturally content. But make certain the situation is not wet in winter since here in the north plants sometimes suffer injury under such conditions.

If you include this iris in occasional sentinel clumps, as I do, through the border you will find the yellow lupine-like *Thermopsis caroliniana* a pleasing companion. I have also liked a white variety of *kaempferi* like Betty F. Holmes, or one of the lavender blues such as Amethyst or Azure with yellow meadowrue, *Thalictrum glaucum,* Bristol Fairy babysbreath, regal lilies and deep purple petunias. To make certain of fine flowering in the border all through the spring and up to blooming time let the slow-running hose rest for several hours weekly among the plants unless, of course, there is heavy rainfall.

Each year notice then the quality of the blossoms. If with good culture these tend to get smaller and stems shorter, you had better decide upon division. This is usually advisable every three or four years, preferably just after flowering in July but any time before October is safe if a later date is more convenient for you. Separate each large clump into two or three sections, not into single pieces, or you will lack flowers completely for the next year or so. Water well following division to stimulate strong rooting before frost.

From winter *stylosa* to midsummer *kaempferi* is a long and entrancing iris season; not too long, however, for us who have tried out iris values in the garden over many years and never found them disappointing. Omit the

A Chart of Tall Delectable Iris

White	Lavender to "Blue"	Dark Blue to Purple	Pink	Maroon	Yellow	Blends
			May			
Crystal Beauty 50″	Gloriole 42″ (light)	Blue Gown 48″	Fascination 48″	Beowulf 32″	Desert Gold 35″	
Los Angeles 40″ (blue-edged)	Shining Waters 42″ (fragrant)		Frieda Mohr 42″		Fair Elaine 38″ (cream and gold)	
		Indian Hills 38″				
					Noonday 40″ (pale)	
			Late May and June			
	Fair Sky 40″ (pale, fragrant)	Blue Velvet 46″	Eros 42″	Dauntless 40″	Alta California 46″	Angelus 36″
Gudrun 42″	Great Lakes 48″	Missouri 44″ (fragrant)	Morocco Rose 36″	The Red Douglas 38″	California Gold 36″	China Maid 40″
Mt. Washington 50″	Princess Beatrice 54″ (fragrant)	The Bishop 38″ (very dark)	Pink Satin 46″	Red Velvet 44″	Eclador 42″	Copper Lustre 42″
	Sensation 48″ (pale)				Naranja 40″ (orange)	Depute Nomblot 48″
Snowdrop 30″	Sierra Blue 48″				Shining Sun 40″	Prairie Sunset 36″
Venus de Milo 36″						

odd little species if you will, but consider indispensable Siberian, oriental and both intermediate and tall bearded varieties. For iris not only affords the border weeks of rich, pure color but its foliage gives strength to the garden composition throughout the entire growing season.

2. Peonies Attract Everyone

When, late in May, my hedge of peonies comes into bloom along the far boundary of the garden, I consider it with the deepest satisfaction. Before this garden was mine, these handsome white flowers, red-flecked and fragrant, gave pleasure to those who loved this place before me, and it may be that when it passes into other hands, divisions of these same peonies will continue year after year to dispense sweetness on the May breeze. For peonies are plants with a delightful present and a long future.

Even the old-fashioned "piney" of colonial days, *Paeonia officinalis,* is a pretty, fragrant thing and likewise the fern-leafed peony, *Paeonia tenuifolia,* which inaugurates the season in early May. A charming single, it has no tendency to purple in its fading days. For cutting, I particularly like this species, which I place each spring in a tall translucent blue jar on the hall lowboy. It is pleasant, I think, to repeat satisfactory bouquets. Familiarity seems, indeed, to make the same arrangements in the same seasons as dear to this household as old tunes.

A good way to learn about peonies is to obtain a catalogue from a firm specializing in them. Here you can study the descriptions according to color and season and note the ratings which the American Peony Society has made on a scale of ten. You will find listed along with hundreds of varieties, a few of the species such as I have enjoyed. These will start the season about a month early for you who love peonies and want them a long while.

The species are not so handsome, however, as the familiar Chinese doubles, which in early, midseason and late varieties offer such a wealth of exquisite form, color and sometimes fragrance too. If you want a scented half dozen moderate-priced but outstanding kinds of these to cover the full season, consider first two earlies—the White Festiva Maxima, a ninety-year-old variety which still holds its own with a 9.3 rating, and the silvery rose Mons. Jules Elie. For midseason Marie Crousse is pale rose-shaded pink, and Mary Brand a handsome crimson. Let the procession end with the soft pink La France and the creamy Enchanteresse. If you are an experienced gardener and willing to take great pains with culture, consider also Le Cygne, Solange and Therese. Not fragrant, these are extremely beautiful varieties, though hardly for the casual gardener.

Among singles there are two outstanding groups. The Japanese or anemone types, with thick golden petaloids forming a high crested center, include three very beautiful midseason varieties—the white Isani Gidui, rose-pink Tokio and crimson Mikado. The other class of singles has a less prominent center and is even lovelier in varieties like the shell-pink Helen, pure white Le Jour and soft pink Pride of Langport, all of which are rare enough still to be fairly expensive.

You will want to investigate also a new race of peonies which flowers ahead of the Chinese doubles and is for the most part single in form. Professor A. P. Saunders of Clinton, New York, has introduced the early and late Windflower with fernlike foliage and beauteous white anemone blooms, the whites Requiem and Chalice, the coral Dainty Lass and salmon-pink Janice. To those of you whose hobby is peonies, these as well as the hybrids of Mr. Lyman Glasscock of Elwood, Illinois, will add a fascinating something new to your plantings.

Peonies in the garden have many values. If their primary use is for bouquets, one plant each of an early, midseason and late variety in favorite colors, plus one or two species may be set out in a cutting row. These will flower from early May through June. For boundaries or low hedges one variety looks best, unless the line is long. Then it may be composed of groups of different colors but all blooming at the same season. For example, a fairly inexpensive, early boundary could be made of simultaneous white, blush and rose loveliness with groups of Duchesse de Nemours, Judge Berry and Mons. Jules Elie or a fairly dear one-color effect for midseason obtained from the very handsome red Philippe Rivoire or gleaming white Kelway's Glorious.

In the perennial border, peonies make fine accents and with their excellent foliage look well there throughout the season. I like the singles for the border perhaps better than the doubles because they are less massive when in bloom and the flowers are light enough to hold up proud heads unassisted after driving summer rain. The white Isani Gidui, for example, is stunning with a tall yellow iris like Alta California behind it and clusters of forget-me-not anchusa for foreground. The single pink Nymph is charming with iris Sensation and the low, lavender Colorado columbine, *Aquilegia caerulea.*

The double pink peony Sarah Bernhardt in the border is well companioned by such a tall *Iris sibirica* as the bright blue Mountain Lake, with low *Nepeta mussini* before it. If the pink Dr. Van Fleet climbing rose grows in the garden, try this group in front of it for June beauty. With the creamy yellow peony Primevere plant the blue bearded iris Shining Waters and oriental poppy Mrs. Perry. This results in pure enchantment if a deep blue carpet of viola Jersey Gem is laid before it. Broad masses of blue baptisia, yellow thermopsis and the white and fragrant garden heliotrope, *Valeriana officinalis,* also form pleasing backgrounds for peonies.

Peonies in the bounteous period of spring flowering may thus be used in innumerable beautiful combinations with iris and columbine but they also look well in beds by themselves. And these can be prominently placed since the foliage from rosy April point to final September green is always of handsome quality. If you plant these perennials near the house, however, by all means select varieties with the added blessing of fragrance. Scent is an important criterion for cutting, too. Pale varieties are especially good to select for cutting since many hold their pastel tones only when cut in the bud and brought indoors.

Well-rooted two-year-old stock containing three to five eyes is the only reliable kind to buy and mid-September to early October the best time to plant. A rich, well-drained soil is essential and a location in full sun for half the day or longer, except for the pale pinks which retain their colors better in light shade. Dig the beds deeply, two feet if you can manage it, for this quite permanent planting. Mix in manure liberally but beyond the immediate range of roots. Let an area of loose sweet soil, either clayey or sandy, surround the crowns and the existing root system. Manure—so important to vigor—is thus kept from direct contact because it seems to be connected with the presence of botrytis blight. Leaf mold is a good thing to combine with the soil around each crown.

When you set out new peonies, place the growing points just below the soil surface so that the buds will be but two inches deep in a firm clay loam and no more than three in a lighter, more open soil. Reserve three to five feet for the full development of each plant. (You can use the space between for a planting of early narcissus.) If you cannot allow two safe weeks between spading and planting, soak the new bed thoroughly to hasten settling. Sinking is dangerous afterwards since it results in the burial of crowns which should remain near the surface.

Take all possible care with this planting operation. Hollow out sufficiently large holes for each clump and work the soil firmly around the roots so as to leave no air pockets. Finally tramp the soil down well and water deeply. Remember you are not planting a perennial which is to be reset in a year or so but one which is to dwell in the same place for five to ten years.

When in the course of time it is necessary to divide, choose a new location or else remove the exhausted soil in the present one and replace it with fresh before resetting the stock. Separate clumps with a sharp knife into strong natural divisions containing at least three growing points. Don't hesitate to discard very old material since this seldom yields worth-while stock.

In October as a sanitary measure, cut off all peony foliage and burn it. Then work a trowelful of bone meal into the soil around each crown. Except for the first year, provide no winter covering.

In the spring, as new growth appears, dust from the time it is a few inches high until buds appear with powdered bordeaux mixture, that is, if your plants have previously been a disappointment. This dusting seems to be a reliable check for the blight which results in the drying up or blasting of buds. Many plantings, of course, are never so affected. A trowelful of wood ashes and of sheep manure at this time supplements the autumn bone meal and in all affords for an average-size plant a very square meal indeed. Peonies of great size or peonies which are being reconditioned can do with three times as much food. Or if a complete fertilizer is being used in the garden the peonies can be given this in spring. In any case it is doubtful if there ever was an over-fed peony plant.

Another spring chore is disbudding. If the size of the flowers is important for cutting or close inspection, by all means remove the two side buds as each group of three forms. If your plants are to be seen at some distance, however, as mine are, don't disbud at all and the flowering period will last longer and be more effective too.

By all means put supports in place early. I always thrust the double-ring tripods around the peonies when growth first appears. Otherwise I find myself so overwhelmed with the spring rush that suddenly the peonies are in full and heavy bloom and handling them then is a terrific chore involving not me alone but two of us. Incidentally, don't worry over ants on the buds. They are after the honey exuding there and doing no harm at all.

Perhaps you are not merely so keen as I am on peonies because for you they have been plants which simply will not bloom. Don't give them up on this account. There is a good reason for this condition which you are sure to be able to remedy.

If plants are in deep shade or growing where they must compete for food and moisture with tree and shrub roots, by all means transplant them to an open, sunny location where very likely they will start to bloom after a year's residence. If you suspect that they have been planted deeper than the allowed two to three inches, reset them. If they are very old plants in a starved condition, you might try to revive them with generous spring and autumn doses of plant food but replacing them with a few stalwart new plants will give you a lot more satisfaction.

If buds drop prematurely and stems discolor or rot off at the base, or if buds turn brown while small, suspect botrytis blight and dust accordingly. A further precaution would be to remove carefully the soil from around the crowns to a depth of two to three inches and to replace it with new. And then to prevent the spread of trouble in the spring, cut off imperfect buds as well as any open flowers just before they shatter, into a paper bag. Then burn it.

Sometimes failing plants reveal, on examination of roots, galls or knots which pathologists say are caused by nematodes. If such roots are dug up and immersed for thirty minutes in water heated to one hundred twenty degrees Fahrenheit they may be saved. Crown and root rot can be similarly checked, the sterilized plants then being reset in fresh soil and preferably in a new location. Only I confess if I had to do all this I'd just throw the plants out and either get a few new ones or conclude there were other perennials for me.

Chinese Peonies of Great Beauty and Easy Culture

Name	Color	Season	Rating	Fragrant
Baroness Schroeder	blush to white	late	9.0	√
Duchesse de Nemours	sulphur white	early	8.1	
Enchanteresse	creamy white	late	8.9	√
Felix Crousse	rose red	mid	8.4	√
Festiva Maxima	red-flecked white	early	9.3	√
Kelway's Glorious	iridescent white	mid	9.8	√
La France	soft pink	late	9.0	√
Longfellow	brightest red	mid	9.0	√
Marie Crousse	salmon pink	mid	8.9	
Mary Brand	crimson	mid	8.7	√
Mons. Jules Elie	silvery pink	early	9.2	
Philippe Rivoire	crimson	mid	9.2	√
Mme. Jules Dessert	flesh	late	9.4	
Sarah Bernhardt	apple blossom pink	late	9.0	
Walter Faxon	pure rose	mid	9.3	

Finally your peonies may not bloom because they are too small and young. The first year after they have been planted, flowering is always meager. If the divisions you set out included less than three eyes, there may be no bloom for a year or two. Quite obviously then, your only remedy is an attitude of patient anticipation. But when they are in full swing and healthy, you will find they have been well worth awaiting, for they are handsome plants, indeed, in or out of bloom, and there is never a shabby spring to autumn moment on the peony calendar.

3. Those Elegant Tree Peonies

TREE peonies are garden aristocrats, expensive and worth it. Like antiques in your house, established tree peonies in the garden are a delight which continues not for seasons alone nor for years but actually for generations. Here in some Philadelphia gardens which date back to the Revolution are tree peonies known to be a century old. Others are upstarts tracing their origins only to the Centennial Exposition of 1876. All, like true philosophers, however, have gained in beauty with age and have refused to succumb to the rigors of fate.

The tree peony is so called because, unlike the familiar herbaceous varieties, it retains a woody framework through the winter. Actually it is a shrub rather than a perennial but its value in the garden is similar to that of perennials. In maturity it grows to three or four feet with a spread of about the same distance. Blooms are actually seven to ten inches across and average twenty-five to one hundred and twenty-five to a plant. There are even record specimens bearing four hundred blooms but no such abundance is necessary for a handsome showing. If in your garden two dozen or so flowers appear on a single specimen I am sure you will be well content.

For these unusual plants are arresting in appearance. In fact, they are inevitable conversation pieces, as attractive to every visitor as they were to the explorer Farrar who first saw them in their native state in Kansu, China, above the Blackwater Valley and later high up near the border of Tibet. "The most overpoweringly superb of shrubs" he excitedly exclaimed as he beheld "on the eaves of the world" this magnificent *Paeonia moutan* in all its grandeur as a wild plant.

Because tree peonies are destined to give you long delight, you will want to make selection with great care. And incidentally a good way to obtain them is as a Christmas or birthday gift. Your husband is bound to consider these a respectable present as he won't the item I mentioned earlier. I hope that you can choose your plants while they are still in bloom and so reserve them in the colors you see instead of the ones you are told about. Where familiar peony varieties flower by Decoration Day, tree peonies may be inspected from May 10 until about May 20. Then the middle of September is the best time to have your reserved plants delivered.

Within the three general types are included varieties in every color but blue. The European or Chinese tree peonies have broad foliage and large, heavy, double blooms. The Japanese are characterized by fine narrow leaves and large, broad-petaled crinkle-tipped single or semi-double flowers displaying a prominent cushion of golden anthers. The finest, most luminous whites are in this class and here you will do well to make your first selection. The yellow *lutea* or Lemoine hybrids, the third type, are the result of the newest crosses of *moutan* varieties with the species *lutea*. Here are the pure yellows and yellow to red tones on plants which are hardy but slow to propagate and therefore comparatively rare, although some growers have recently brought them down considerably in price.

All of these tree peonies—Chinese, Japanese and *lutea* —are available in five-inch pots. They flower the second year after planting. Field-grown plants, ready to bloom immediately, cost just twice as much, since they are twice as old. Getting them safely through their first years takes care. Once they are happily established, they usually stay so.

Among the European tree peonies Reine Elizabeth, which the horticulturist John Wister terms "the finest of all Chinese doubles," is a lovely cherry rose. It is plentiful, an older hybrid and therefore low in price. Bijou de Chusan is a delicate blush pink. Comtesse de Tuder and Carolina d'Italie are excellent pale pinks, and Marquise de Clapiers, a vivid salmon. I do not recommend to you the sturdy, undistinguished but very available pink Banksi which beside other pinks is "absolute rubbish" or Athlete, which is a "dirty magenta."

Considered more beautiful by many enthusiasts are the less heavily petaled Japanese whites like Snow White,

Moonbeam and the fragrant, quite double Renkaku or Rein-Kaku, meaning Flight of Cranes. King of the Peonies is a magnificent semi-double rose and Rimpo, a stunning royal purple. Fugi-No-Mori or Orchid is another beauty. Generally speaking, all of these flower more freely than the Chinese and require less staking.

Among the *lutea* hybrids Argosy is first class, also La Lorraine, and both are fragrant. Souvenir de Maxine Cornu inclines to too much purple suffusion and often hangs its head. Mme. Louis Henry has a fine cup-shaped form with noticeably waved petals. It appeals to those who like buff, pink and copper tones in one bloom rather than the purer soft sulphur yellow of La Lorraine.

As with herbaceous peonies, the tree peonies are set out in mid-September or seven to ten days earlier in those regions where first frosts are likely to occur before mid-October. Browning of foliage is a good indication of ripeness for moving and a month in the new place before frost is the aim. Full sun used to be considered essential to free flowering, but Mr. Wister finds his plants in partial shade doing even better than those in the open. An evergreen planting or similar shield behind tree peonies protects them from the full sweep of the wind and forms a barrier to the late touch of frost.

Since such peonies are permanent assets, beds or individual planting holes are deeply dug, as they are for herbaceous peonies, and the soil similarly improved. If it is on the stiff, rather heavy side so much the better. Don't, of course, cut back the tough top growth. Indeed, the development of a tall, free-branching frame is now your object. On the strength of this depends the abundance of the crop.

One of the pleasantest attributes of tree peonies is their earliness of bloom. Near May 6 the pageant commences, *Paeonia moutan*, the species, holding the lead. Long before Decoration Day, while the herbaceous peonies are only just making up their minds, the tree peonies adorn their woody branches with the choicest blooms the garden ever produces. A single plant, accenting an important point in a shrubbery boundary planting, is arresting. Two as sentinels at the garden gate are attractive. Four in the corners of a formal garden are elegantly important, while a whole row edging drive or walk make every visitor exclaim at the beauty of a plant which supersedes even the grandeur of the finest herbaceous peonies and appears weeks ahead of them, at that.

But a row of tree peonies! Well, that idea makes us budget-conscious gardeners gasp until we try our hands at propagation. Then we can count on one or two purchased plants developing, in the course of time, into twelve or eighteen. A ten-year-old plant, for example, may be lifted and divided. Sometimes a clump readily falls apart. In other cases it is necessary to cut through the roots with a saw. This can be successfully accomplished.

But there is another way to propagate. After your bought plant has reached four- to five-year-old, flowering size, start propagating in September. For this business turn first to your herbaceous peonies, since these provide the first root system on which pieces of tree peony tops will establish themselves. Any varieties of herbaceous peonies will do but avoid species plants since these are only determined about propagating themselves.

Begin by lifting with a spading fork a clump of herbaceous peonies. Let it lie in the sun for twenty-four hours. This limbers up the fleshy roots. Next cut these into six-inch lengths. (You can then return the herbaceous peony to its former dwelling place where it will take up its old habits, little the worse for its experience in the open.)

Now cut three-inch lengths of tree-peony wood from the tops of the specimen you bought. Allow at least two leaf buds to each piece. With a sharp knife slice away one inch of bark from the *lower* end of each of these tree peony cuttings. Slice away also one inch from the *upper* part of one side of the herbaceous root cuttings. Lay the tree peony and the herbaceous peony roots so that the cut parts are side by side, cambium tissue next to cambium. Then tie these sections firmly together with raffia and cover with melted candle or grafting wax.

In a garden bed where drainage is absolutely assured, plant the grafted pieces in a row. Space them twelve inches apart and insert deeply enough to cover completely each of their tops. Now nothing will be visible of the new tree peony planting until the following spring when green shoots will appear and develop. Finally let two full years pass before transplanting the young tree peonies from this nursery row to their permanent locations. One hundred percent success will, of course, not be probable, but if you manage the average forty percent you will still be getting a big increase.

During these two years the youngster tree peonies will

develop single stems some twelve inches long. A mass of lead-pencil roots of their own nature will also be developing above and around the herbaceous roots which nourished the grafted twigs at the start. After the second year, lift this nursery stock, and cut away the herbaceous roots entirely. Then replant your personally developed stock in its permanent location, setting the plants some two or three inches deeper than they grew before. Such deeper planting encourages the further development of roots.

Obviously such propagation is not recommended except for really patient and energetic gardeners to whom the propagating of plants is as great a joy as the sight of the finished flowering product. The moderately patient must, of course, dig into their pockets and buy all their plants, while the truly impatient are strongly advised to eschew tree peonies entirely, and stick to daylilies, iris and other plants of immediate result.

Impatient gardeners will thus miss a lot. Like certain other blessings of life, however, which the patient savor and the impatient forego, they probably won't guess how much, unless they happen to come upon your row of dazzling pink Reine Elizabeth or royal purple Bird of Rimpow plants some bright May morning, when these are putting on what might, horticulturally speaking, be described as the greatest show on earth.

4. Oriental Poppies Sparkle

As SPRING slips into summer, the oriental poppies open crinkled silken cups of glowing pink, blazing red or shining white. As brilliant in this early season as phlox is later, these poppies from mid-May to mid-June make a garden sing with color. They need a careful setting, however, or the song goes out of tune, with flaming orange protecting the propinquity of rose or a patch of cerise defending itself against yellow.

Do not on this account omit poppies unless your border or garden is quite small so that you can not afford to reserve space for this plant of ten days bloom and six weeks disappearance. For a well-grown poppy does require room, almost as much, in fact, as a peony clump. Furthermore, in border settings you must place before it some plant of more constant quality to cover its long summer retreat. I have liked for this purpose Chinese delphinium, shasta daisies or tall annual snapdragons. I secure these from the florist as blooming-size plants in order to have them ready early enough for this cover-up role.

In ten-foot or wider borders problems of masking can be readily solved. Or elsewhere in the garden you can plan for a separate bed of oriental poppies. This may be edged with August lilies if a lightly shaded location is selected for the lovely lilac-rose Enchantress or old rose-toned Henri Cayeux which hold their colors better out of the sun. Or a phlox variety may be interplanted with the poppy. This is a good plan since many a brilliant summer phlox is better gleaming by itself than in the intimate harmonies of a thick-set border.

In the border you will probably prefer the paler poppies like the dwarf, early Little Shrimp, Barr's White or the various pink ones. The salmon Olympia, often the first to bloom, is charming with white iris Crystal Beauty. Use forget-me-not anchusa in the foreground and then, if you can, place your entire masterpiece before such a climbing rose as the creamy Gardenia. Helen Elizabeth is an enchanting midseason pink poppy to plant with madonna lilies and early delphinium or other June blues such as the tall Dropmore anchusa, which is a less usual but delightful poppy companion.

Mrs. Perry is the first of the pinks most of us grew. Early in June it is utterly lovely with pale and deeper blue iris or those like the golden Shining Sun or creamy pink Midgard which pick up the yellow subtleties of its salmon shadings. Or for brilliant effect plant a lustrous red oriental poppy like Trilby with the creamy peony Primevere, and the Siberian iris Blue Flame.

In time you will, of course, work out perfect poppy pictures of your own. In planning consider that Olympia, May Queen, Henri Cayeux, Little Shrimp, Prince of Orange and Mary Ellen bloom early, that is, within the first ten days of poppy season. In the last ten days appear Wunderkind, Snowflame, Gold of Ophir, Sass Pink and Perfection. The others—making up the poppy majority—are midseason, carrying May into June. Flowers stay fresh three to four days, the late ones not quite so long as the earlies. Agreeable companions are columbine, pyrethrum and flax, foxgloves, canterbury bells, garden heliotrope, early delphinium and iris.

The tall, blood red Australia or the cerise Wunderkind or the cherry Joyce you may prefer by themselves although they look well, too, combined with Barr's White or the soft contrasting grays of artemisia Silver King or *Gypsophila paniculata.* Perhaps you will set Chinese red Mandarin in its own stark beauty before a backdrop of yew. One gardener found it harmonious with Sierra Blue and yellow Eclador iris, the Winsome daylily and a few white shastas. Another preferred to see her favorite deep glowing reds with a background of such white June shrubs as mock orange, weigela or snowball.

But no matter what the varieties of oriental poppy you select you will discover that they are winter hardy, thrifty and undemanding. In fact, if your garden were all poppies you wouldn't need spray or dust gun, hose or fertilizers, which only induce rank growth. At planting time set the crowns at a forty-five degree angle. This is a safety measure to avoid crown rot from standing water. Cover with a three-inch layer of soil. So planted in a sunny garden bed, well-drained and originally well-prepared with leaf mold and bone meal, poppies can be trusted to carry on beautifully by themselves for many years.

That doesn't mean, however, that you can't change your mind about their location and switch them around occasionally the way we women do most of our garden flowers. It is just an old wives' tale that oriental poppies can't be transplanted. Take with them the same safeguarding ball of earth you do with other large perennials and you will discover not only that your big poppies do not object to transition but that in the locality they left, there is coming along quite a crop of offspring.

For poppies are great breeders. Wherever a bit of root

remains, there a poppy plant springs up. Therefore, if you have a favorite variety, you can count on bounteous propagation by the simple method of root cuttings explained before (see page 64).

Mid-July to late September is the time for drastic poppy dealings. After their spring exuberance these perennials drop off to sleep like tired kittens. Keep their locations well marked then and don't let other perennials or annuals crowd in on them through July and early August because before that month is over, each plant will wake from its deep sleep and produce a crisp, fresh crown of leaves. When this is well in evidence you can divide or transplant or take root cuttings. Of course, don't disturb happily located, flourishing plants unless you have a reason. Like many other perennials poppies prefer untravelled intervals of three to five years.

If you are setting new poppies out in spring, obtain pot-grown plants. In late summer and fall, field-grown clumps will move well. Allow a generous eighteen-inch space for either. A mulch is required the first winter. A thin layer of straw, excelsior or peat moss will do. Pull the material under, never over, the persisting foliage. In spring watch out for heaving. Those poppy crowns want the protection of two or three inches of soil. Their second year, no winter covering is needed.

Unless you have recently experimented with them, you may be surprised to learn that you no longer need to write poppies off as cut flowers. The pink variety, Betty Anne, is particularly good for bouquets because it flowers so abundantly and seems to last longer when cut than any other variety. Where a great shock of color looks well indoors, as on the grand piano or at the shuttered landing window, no arrangement will give you greater pleasure than one of oriental poppies. These are not, however, flowers for casual cutting. You must gather them just as the buds show color and before the bees get to them either in the evening or early morning. Sear the stems as promptly as possible over a gas flame until the lower inch or so is charred.

A Full Season of Brilliant Poppies

Variety	Color	Height in Inches	Season
Australia	Spectrum red	42	mid
Barr's White	Pure white with dark spots	30	mid
Echo	Silvery pink, maroon spotted	30	mid
Enchantress	Lilac rose	34	mid
Helen Elizabeth	La France pink, no spots	24	mid
Henri Cayeux	Old rose	30	early
Joyce	Cherry red	48	mid
Little Shrimp	Shrimp pink	18	early
Olympia	Salmon	24	early
Mrs. Perry	Salmon	29	mid
Snowflame	Yellow and white bicolor	30	late
Wunderkind	Cerise	33	late

Or follow my plan of taking a lighted candle and a pail of water to the garden for poppy cutting at dusk. I sear each stem as I cut and immediately plunge it up to the neck of the flower in the water. The pail is placed on the porch for the night and next to the house wall where no early eastern sun will touch the poppy buds. Indoors then in the morning the bouquet is arranged. The buds open their glowing chalices quickly and the flowers stay fresh four days or more.

Six-inch blossoms, two- to four-foot plants, colors that make of the rainbow a pallid arc and a month's succession of cut flowers—all this, with less than usual routine care, makes the oriental poppy a perennial prized by every knowing gardener whose space permits its brilliant habitation.

CHAPTER VIII

IMPORTANT PERENNIALS FOR SUMMER

1. Phlox, Song of Summer

THE flowering of phlox is a sign of summer. When in my borders the white Miss Lingard perfects its scented blooms, I know that warm days are near at hand and that with them comes one of the most glorious and lavish of perennial displays. For phlox is no modest, shrinking subject, to be sought out and appreciated in a shady nook.

Flamboyant, friendly and sun-loving, as American as a milk shake, it flaunts its brilliant midseason colors in any well-tended garden. Even in deserted country dooryards it may be seen in every shade of rose, purple and white, neglected yet beautiful, with the gray weather-beaten walls of some forsaken homestead for background. Obviously self-reliant and persistent, such seedling descendants of hardy phlox set out years before do not readily succumb to the blows of fate.

Wise, indeed, is the gardener who reserves space for lavish dealings with phlox, especially if summers are spent at home. But when plans are made to use this perennial either in a garden of its own or in a mixed border, certain facts about it are to be kept in mind. The tall early *Phlox suffruticosa,* Miss Lingard, with shining leaf and fragrant flower, gives a June effect ahead of the more diversified *paniculatas* and will keep flowering right into October. "The best perennial of all perennials," one wise plantsman justly described it. You will find Miss Lingard effective with delphinium blues and salmon sweet william. Avoid the pink Miss Verboom in this class. It tends to be a difficult magenta. Following the bloom of Lingard phlox the dwarf white Mia Ruys looks well in a foreground position.

The July and August *Phlox paniculata* varies in height from this fifteen-inch dwarf to the tall and handsome, forty-inch E. I. Farrington. The *paniculata* season extends here from the end of June to the second or third week in October. Colors are so brilliant and clashing in this group that varieties must be selected with caution and grouped with care. There can be no artless beauty achieved by the careless flinging about of phlox. To make certain of pleasing effects I first grow unfamiliar varieties in a separate row-by-row bed. Here I check up on colors and find out which goes with which, according to my taste, before introducing them to the on-view border.

In my test plot I also note quality of plant. I found that Columbia was the prettiest true pink imaginable but, alas, of too weak stem quality. I discovered that the brilliant violets like Blue Boy were better alone or with gray-leaved perennials. I noted that E. I. Farrington and

Charles Curtis were salmon shades of real glory and that the cherry Augusta used sparingly among rose pinks gave them a real lift. I found that the whites with a rose eye like Count Zeppelin, of incessant bloom, and Europa were something special, although no catalogue description had ever moved me in their favor. Painted Lady I triple checked for the pale silvery rose beauty of its excellent blooms.

As you examine phlox colors you will see that there are no true reds nor true blues. The so-called blues all have a rose cast which makes them count as lavender or purple. The pinks are of two kinds, rose with a tinge of blue and salmon with a hint of yellow. If you keep in mind these supplementary color values, you can select phlox companions far more effectively. Thus the tall early, yellow-red Leo Schlageter looks well with such a daylily as the pale yellow Hyperion or the meadowrue *Thalictrum glaucum*. Gaillardia Mr. Sherbrook and the Yellow Supreme marigold will be pleasing companions to such later varieties as Salmon Glow and Salmon Beauty. The soft rose-pink Enchantress will be right with hardy aster Blue Gem, or with lavender hostas. With Harvest Fire, one of the most brilliant of all phlox varieties, plant white regal lilies and misty clouds of babysbreath. And for peacemaking amidst the rival brilliance of purple, rose or salmon phlox it is not necessary always to resort to blush or white varieties. You may select one of the placating gray-foliaged perennials like artemisia Silver King or *Gypsophila paniculata*.

If part of the phlox border is to pass under the open

shade of trees so much the better. In light shadow set the lavenders and purples which there will not go magenta as they fade, and the rose pinks too, since they have the same tendency in brilliant sunshine. But do not use for an edging in the shade the dwarf *Phlox subulata*, which requires the sun not only for flowering but actually to sustain life. Consider also for shadowed locations plantings of the *Phlox arendsi* hybrids. These eighteen-inch crosses between the lovely wild spring species, *divaricata*, and the summer *paniculata*, where they are content, tend to flower continuously from spring into autumn. The soft silvery lilac of Hilda looks very nice to the fore of the first lavender drift of a phlox border.

Even in a modest suburban place phlox can be planted to create a superb effect. I think of one garden where it has been used predominantly along the entire hundred and twenty-five-foot length of the lawn. Here a Virginia fence affords interesting background contrast to the vertical phlox plants which occupy almost exclusively the eight-foot-deep border. A minimum of supplementary material gives other seasonal values. Since the scheme of this display is easy to duplicate I shall outline it here.

Phlox subulata, Maysnow, makes a charming white April edging. Behind it there are alternating colonies of narcissus Aerolite (yellow) and Bernardino (white and yellow) and tulips Clara Butt (pink) and Reverend Ewbank (lavender) with a small planting of the lavender dwarf spring *Phlox divaricata* separating each bulb group. Before the bulbs die down, small plants of white lantana from the florist are inserted among them. After this spring picture, come the drifting masses of summer *Phlox decussata*, or *paniculata* as it is often called, meaning of upright panicle.

Commencing with lavender and purple shades, a progression of color has been worked out from the terrace, the spot from which the garden is usually enjoyed. The pale and safe Antonin Mercier is here grouped with the deeper Maid Marian and Progress, the strongest color there. Next comes a long wave of two pale varieties, Count Zeppelin and Europa which really are whites with rose eyes but count as blush a short distance from the terrace. (A group of Atlanta with a blue eye could be substituted.)

These blend into a mass of rose pinks, Painted Lady and Apple Blossom with the lower growing Cameron to the fore of this group. Three fine whites, the midseason Mrs. Jenkins and the taller late Marie Louise compose the next group with the early Mia Ruys to the fore. These are for blending since the border is terminated beyond them by the salmon pinks in varieties brilliant as a desert sunset. The medium high Salmon Beauty here blends into the taller and deeper E. I. Farrington, and Leo Schlageter, the nearest to red.

This garden of *paniculata* phlox carries on all through the summer and far into fall, flowering repeatedly from new growth, as the first and finest blooms are consistently removed at the base of the fading flower head. In autumn, the garden is again supplemented with hardy asters. In this particular border the lavender variety, gay Border Blue, is set behind the white and blush phlox and the white Mt. Everest behind the lavender, rose and salmon-pink varieties. Thus this wide border holds color from April almost to frost.

In my garden it is the white varieties—Miss Lingard, Mrs. Jenkins and Marie Louise—which have given me particular pleasure. On moonlit evenings, these shine out luminous and lovely dispensing a sweet fragrance. Coolly beautiful, the sight of them is refreshing on the most humid night.

I also find phlox a charming landscape plant. One enchanting colony is effectively set in a small green and white plot which is primarily a bird sanctuary. For background, there is a graceful hemlock and a clump of hybrid rhododendrons. To the fore rise strong clumps of Miss Lingard with an underplanting of lily-of-the-valley. In the midst stands the bird bath. From June on, it is the white phlox which makes intermittently lovely this quiet spot at the end of the vista from my study window.

Culturally speaking, phlox does well in full sun or in moderate, open shade. Out of the glare, colors are truer, especially in the blue varieties. Plants keep both health and looks in either situation if the soil is rich, deeply prepared and well drained, and the planting uncrowded. Deep watering in times of drought is essential but overhead sprinkling is to be avoided.

It is also most important that each plant be allowed a full fifteen-inch area with a free circulation of air about it. The ills the phlox is heir to are kept at a minimum under proper growing conditions. Often they do not put in an appearance at all. There are two principal deterrents. Foliage sometimes appears rusty with leaves curling under. This indicates red spider. A strong hose spray directed from below the plant frequently suffices to break the tough spider webs and wash away the minute offenders. Or dusting sulphur may be regularly applied. Sulphur has a double value if humid days bring the second ailment, mildew, which disfigures the plants although it does little harm. The sulphur is, of course, kept as much as possible away from flower heads because it ruins color, especially reds.

Phlox does not, as is commonly supposed, revert in color. When lovely blues or pinks seem to change to magenta, it is because faded blooms have been permitted to go to seed and the lusty seedlings, which do not come true, have crowded out the parent plant. "Reversion" is prevented by prompt removal of blooms past their prime, by adequate feeding and by frequent enough division to keep the centers of the plant in a healthy growing condition. This means about every third year.

September is an excellent time for separating phlox. Center parts are then discarded and strong outside sections cut apart with a knife rather than a spade, into three to five budded divisions. These are then reset at the same height they grew before but in well-forked and much-enriched soil and at proper fifteen-inch distances. If this task is completed three to four weeks before the first frost, new roots firmly anchor the fresh divisions and next year's display is lavish despite the disturbance.

Since hybrid phlox does not come true from seeds, plantings are increased either by such divisions or by cuttings. It is, indeed, a simple matter to get a fine crop of some favorite like the still fairly expensive Marie Louise if you will take tip cuttings in July or August. I have had them form good roots in three weeks.

If size of bloom is an objective, remove at the stem line from each strong phlox clump all but about five main shoots. These will then produce big heads of bloom.

Guides through the Phlox Maze

(Varieties of *P. decussata* are Early, commencing late June or the beginning of July; Midseason, in mid-July; Late, at the end of July.)

Variety	Color	Season	Comment
Antonin Mercier	Pale lilac	Early	Safe, pale shade
Blue Boy	Deep violet	Mid	Broad plant
Maid Marian	Pink lavender	Mid	Good blending tone
Progress	Shaded violet	Mid	Clear, deep color
Count Zeppelin	White with rose eye	Early	Marvelous, long blooming
Europa	White with dark eye	Mid	Fine, counts as blush
Cameron (dwarf)	Rose pink	Early	Foreground
Enchantress	Rose pink	Mid	Fine plant
Painted Lady	Silvery pale rose	Mid	Excellent
Apple Blossom	Soft rose pink	Mid	Very large florets
Mrs. Jenkins	Creamy white	Mid	All white
Mia Ruys (dwarf)	Pure white	Early	Fragrant
Marie Louise	Chalk white	Late	Large florets, finest white
Charles Curtis	Glowing salmon	Early	Very fine
E. I. Farrington	Dark salmon	Early	Outstanding large florets
Leo Schlageter	Yellow red	Early	Full pyramidal heads
Salmon Beauty	With white eye	Mid	Very large florets
Harvest Fire	Salmon orange	Mid	Most brilliant of all

For general garden effect, however, this hardly seems worth while, and, of course, phlox is not the perennial for cutting. It falls too readily.

The colors and values of phlox are exciting. The culture is restful. This, I think, is the pleasant combination of attributes which makes certain perennials important.

2. Delphinium, Most Beauteous of Spires

The blue spires of delphinium, like the steeples of churches in country towns, bring even to simple gardens a charming distinction. Whether the blue wands rise in effective isolation from a green base or present the perfect foil to pale yellow daylilies or white masses of phlox, they are always important. Indeed, the delphinium with its "spirited emotional appeal" has no rival for landscape value in the flower garden. And for bouquets it is equally handsome.

But since in our busy lives the behavior of a plant is quite as important as its beauty, we must inquire into the disposition of the delphinium. Is it exacting or is it amiable? Perhaps a charitable dictum would be—it is improving. The delphinium we must realize is basically a native of high altitude and cool climate and there are limits to its powers of adjustment.

Therefore if you live on the Pacific coast or in New England where the heat of summer days is mitigated by cool evenings and humidity is high near the sea, you can expect to bring to perfection the giant hybrid beauties. If, however, your garden is near Philadelphia, or in some sections of the Midwest or around New York City, where the summers are sudden, droughty and blisteringly hot, you can enjoy the handsomest hybrids only if you will be satisfied to have them behave as biennials or even annuals. The sturdy *Delphinium chinense,* and the less spectacular but still very lovely hybrids *D. belladonna* and *D. bellamosum,* will, however, usually prove perennial.

The feathery, thirty-inch blue and white Chinese delphiniums are nice to mass for constant summer bloom. These are the most dependable of all. Easily grown from late April sowings, they blossom their first year early in September when other true blues are scarce.

The three- to four-foot *D. belladonna* flowers abundantly in June, and sometimes through the summer too, and again in September. It is enchanting in the familiar combination with white madonna or *candidum* lilies and with some such climbing rose as Silver Moon or the deeper Coralie for background, a carpeting of salmon sweet william at its feet. A more unusual picture results when against a backdrop of evergreens, *D. belladonna* is companioned by white foxgloves or the pale yellow *Digitalis Isabellina. Delphinium bellamosa* is a deeper blue. Both take five months from seed. Midsummer sowings produce first crops the next summer between the blooming time of the older established plantings.

Whether you live in a favored delphinium section or not, the Wrexham or hollyhock-flowered strain and the Giant Pacific Hybrids will some day entice you. Truly lovely are the light blue Summer Skies series, the dark blue and purple King Arthurs and those handsome glistening whites of the Galahad group. Pink delphiniums are today a further invitation but still not so tempting as the translucent blues.

If you live in one of the difficult delphinium sections, it may be only sensible for you to forego the tedious process of seeding. There is no disgrace, indeed, in considering delphinium as a worth-while yearly garden luxury and each spring purchasing one- and two-year-old plants from a specialist. Usually a few of these survive into the third or even fourth year. Half pull through to the second. Others may succumb by fall especially if summer heat is continuous and intense, or plants are infected by one of the crown rot organisms, the most common cause of a short life span. Even so, these purchased plants will produce at least two and often three glorious periods of bloom. Then if they depart, you can still bless your delphiniums as annuals of extraordinary loveliness.

You may, of course, enjoy the challenge of seeds and the generous crop a successful sowing produces. If so, much advice both simple and intricate confronts you at this point. I have had best results, however, from taking the long way round with delphinium seeds and so follow the method specialists have worked out for us who live in adverse localities.

Obtain fresh seed, they urge, in July or August. Then prepare a florist's flat, the deep kind, with a sifted mixture of two parts good top soil and one part sand. Level the soil off smoothly and firm it well.

Next shake up a pinch of Semesan in each seed packet.

Portfolio

OF

PERENNIAL PLANTS

THEIR PLACEMENTS

IN GARDENS

AND

THEIR ARRANGEMENT

IN THE HOUSE

F. W. Raetz

Spring Symphony. Primroses and narcissus bring early color to borders dominated by the graceful structure and delicate blossoms of a flourishing apple tree.

Gottscho-Schleisner

Snowdrifts in May. The hardy evergreen candytuft, finest of informal edging plants, here mingles with pale yellow alyssum to adorn a low wall.

J. Horace McFarland Co.

Peonies, Luminous and Lovely. In May and June these handsome perennials of sturdy foliage and alluring blossom offer beauty to the garden and bouquets for the house.

J. Horace McFarland Co.

Accent on *Iris.* Late in spring a strong clump of pale bearded iris has compelling charm as its bright flowers open beside a flight of garden steps.

J. Horace McFarland Co.

Poppies Glistening in the Sun. With deutzia for background, these well placed oriental poppy and iris plants again proclaim the pleasing affinity of perennials and shrubs.

Gottscho-Schleisner

Beauty Beside a Pool. In June the great flat blossoms of Japanese iris grace the curving water's edge and thrive there in dampness and sun.

Gottscho-Schleisner

Late Summer in My Garden. With the full blessing of the sun repeated planting units afford bright successive pictures from April to November. Gayfeathers and larkspur, nicotiana and marigold dominate early September.

Gottscho-Schleisner

The Blessings of Shade. Where dappled sunshine filters through the open branches of trees, colonies of scented white astilbes and drifts of pale yellow daylilies brighten June and early July.

Gottscho-Schleisner

Early Garden Dividends. Silhouetted against the dark gleaming patina of an antique desk, this white bowl of spicy grass pinks, pansies and hardy sweet peas is pleasant to gaze on and fragrant to smell.

Gottscho-Schleisner

Basketful of Border Bounty. For the vases in September there are quantities of single and double chrysanthemums, hardy asters, dahlias and marigolds with glistening red berries from the high-bush cranberry shrubs.

Gottscho-Schleisner

Doorway Delight. Phlox, babysbreath and delphinium flower here through summer and fall with spires of gayfeathers appearing in September and always the sweet scent of nicotiana drifting into study and hall.

Gottscho-Schleisner

Daylilies for the Shadows. The lavender hostas with delicate, lily-like panicles and glossy enduring foliage, blossom in filtered sunlight and thrive where other plants fail.

Gottscho-Schleisner

Autumn Greeting for a Guest. In September sprays of white waxen anemones and delicate blue asters gleam in the lamplight to welcome the visitor.

Gottscho-Schleisner

October Favorites. All through the month bold arrangements of shaggy, double yellow, and white, red and bronze single chrysanthemums, with rhododendron foliage, adorn the deep window sills of the living room.

Gottscho-Schleisner

The Indispensable Cold Frame. In this triplex, feverfew plants soon will give place to tender chrysanthemums while one section of young delphiniums and another of foxgloves remain for spring transplanting.

This deters damping off. Sow the seed thickly in rows and directly on the surface of the soil. Press it down firmly with brick or block and cover with a very thin layer of sand.

Now plunge the planted flat part way into water in the kitchen sink or laundry tub. Let it stay until the soil surface feels moist. Then remove the flat to some cool, sheltered place which is light but not sunny and where there is good air circulation. If you have a cool garage or shed this is a better place than on the porch or under the grape arbor.

During the next ten to fourteen days, until germination occurs, water carefully and as frequently as is necessary to keep the soil barely moist. A house plant bulb syringe sprays a finer mist than you can get from the sprinkling can. When true leaves develop, following the first seed leaves, transfer your seedlings to the cold frame.

Here set them four inches apart in a mixture of top soil, sand and leaf mold or commercial humus or compost. Place a lath screen as a shade and prop up or remove the glass top. After the first hard freeze apply a light mulch and place an old window screen over the frame to keep out mice or other unwanteds.

Early in the spring, investigate. When you see growth, remove the mulch and cultivate the bed. As soon as the weather is fairly settled, plant your crop where you want it but until the plants have bloomed, apply no fertilizer.

An unshaded northern site is ideal for mature delphinium plants. Here they will be likely to live far longer than in the full heat of southern or western exposures.

However, if your borders face south, as they are likely to, place your plants where they will give you the most pleasure. And if they grow in the mixed border, trim back through the summer any rampant perennials or lusty annuals which crowd around them and so invite disease by preventing a free circulation of air. In a garden row by themselves, however, I get the best flowers for cutting.

If success with delphinium means a lot to you, you might prepare the soil an ideal three feet deep. But this undoubtedly involves a terrific amount of digging, much more than the average back can bear or the average pocketbook afford. Feel, therefore, that you have done right by your delphinium when in a well-drained spot you improve the soil, with leaf mold or compost and bone meal, to a full eighteen-inch depth. Provide an extra six-inch drainage area if the site requires it. Waterlogged delphiniums, of course, rarely survive.

Two weeks after young plants have bloomed for the first time, around each one, work in and water in a light top dressing of fertilizer. Once in early spring feed your established delphiniums. These incidentally are better off without winter protection, except where the climate is extremely cold. As the first blooms fade, cut the flower stalks down. And after the plants have had a fortnight's rest, sprinkle fertilizer a second time under the outer leaf spread of each one. Cultivate the soil lightly then and water deeply. As new shoots develop, select two or three and pinch back the others. When this second flower crop fades, cut back as before, but do not attempt to force a third period of bloom with further feeding. It may appear anyway.

Meanwhile delphiniums cannot be left unsupported. Before the fatalities of wind or rain occur, firmly insert in the soil wire or bamboo stakes long enough to support the ultimate height of each spire. Fasten these with 'twistems or raffia to the present farthest point of growth.

In summer mulch to keep the root runs cool and so reduce heat and dryness, ever the bane of delphinium. Disease and pest controls are, of course, necessary. A mite sometimes distorts tip growth, particularly if the plants are not too environmentally content. Mildew often appears during humid July days. Certain soil-borne diseases may attack the crowns. By all means lift and burn badly infected plants. But you can prevent many troubles by dusting all leaf surfaces on the first and fifteenth of each month with a sulphur and rotenone preparation.

After this account of the depressing aspects of delphinium culture, let's think again of the great beauty which makes much attention worth while. And, of course, if it does not seem worth while, just skip delphinium. I realize that the longer I garden the less I coddle. In most cases if plants cannot thrive under the average conditions I offer, we simply part. Somehow delphiniums have never invited such independence and so year after year I continue to do my best for them and to enjoy them tremendously.

My first delphinium delight occurs in June when the glorious Pacific Hybrids dominate my borders. Their companions then are the tall pale yellow meadowrue,

Thalictrum glaucum, and the white Miss Lingard phlox with a haze of babysbreath between. White regal lilies, the easiest of all lilies to grow, support this blue delphinium beauty while in the foreground are yellow snapdragons and white and purple petunias, both florist-started annuals. Another pleasing group consists of the white delphinium, Galahad, pink, long-spurred columbines and the yellow evening primrose, *Oenothera missouriensis*.

When after a rest the delphinium spires, not so tall this time, make a second appearance in summer their principle companion is the fragrant white-flowering tobacco, *Nicotiana affinis*. This readily self sows. Therefore, I think of these two as close perennial friends, their blue and white loveliness an appealing summer picture.

But one year a pink nicotiana seedling sprang up beside a rose-centered blue delphinium in a place where blush Gruss an Aachen polyantha roses made an edging. This was an enchanting trio well worth your planning for some year. Delphinium, however, seem to look well with all other flowers. The mock orange, Avalanche, for example, is a beautiful background for belladonna hybrids and pink canterbury bells and in some seasons the luscious mauve of oriental iris appears in time to create a soft harmony of color.

But why should I go on with tantalizing descriptions of this loveliness? There isn't one of you, I know, who doesn't appreciate the beauty of delphiniums. What I wish I could recommend is some certain method for making this cool, independent transient, a really heat-tolerant perennial. When this is discovered, I shall indeed have delphinium news.

3. Daisies Are a Generous Clan

"As COMMON as a daisy" is today a completely outmoded expression. For such distinguished modern compositas as the gerbera, frikarti aster and new gaillardias, to name but a few, now far surpass the artless ox-eye daisies of the field and wild asters of the meadow, and proclaim with the opening of each elegant blossom the plant hunter's courage or the hybridizer's art. Furthermore, these most uncommon daisies are easily grown and may be depended on for long periods of handsome bloom in your borders as well as good keeping qualities for bouquets.

If your garden is small, one or two varieties selected for each season assure progressive color. If it is long with good depth, many compositas result in massive effects of unrivaled brilliance. Singularly free of pest and disease, daisies require more frequent division than many other perennials and more constant picking than the usual run of annuals.

There are two noteworthy perennial daisies for spring and early summer effect—leopardbane, *Doronicum*, and the painted daisy, *Pyrethrum*.

In the apple tree bed in my garden it is *Doronicum caucasicum*, a golden yellow daisy, which with lavender Dream and pink Princess Elizabeth tulips, yellow primroses, hardy white candytuft and deep blue forget-me-not anchusa makes a delightful spring picture. This doronicum, an ideal tulip companion, grows some two feet high, and is so placed that interplantings of white petunias may conceal its July and August dormancy. Unlike most daisies, it grows well in heavy soil either in sun or partial shade and sometimes produces a second crop if first flowers are promptly removed. The earliest of the perennial daisies, these doronicums are well worth investigating for they seem to be rarely grown except for the flower shows.

Pyrethrums are fine for companion groups in the border or for cutting. I like the singles best and prefer plants of Pink Bouquet to face down delphinium, but available seed now seems either to be in mixtures or in the varieties Single Ruby Red and Startler. So I grow the mixture and hold over the pink ones for perennial treatment. These two-foot painted daisies thrive in full sun and rich soil freely mixed with well-rotted manure. They want deep watering in times of drought.

The season is now continued by gaillardias and shasta daisies which are infinitely superior to the grandiflora blanket flowers and white marguerites of an earlier day. Mr. Sherbrook is a notable old gold variety of gaillardia which adds a pleasing, all-season yellow to the garden. I find its curving stems also add interest to any arrangement. Flowering steadily from June to November it is unbelievably drought-resistant and reliable provided it is planted in rich, light soil. In heavy clayey loam it has been for me an unsatisfactory bloomer and rarely survives the winter. G. Ruby is of similar quality in a glowing red. Both these modern gaillardias are true self colors with no detracting flecks or streaks. I prefer them to the familiar coreopsis which seems entirely undistinguished though it does deserve recognition for utter durability and incessant flowering.

When I think of shasta daisies, four of them seem almost indispensable. The thirty-inch Silver Star, an anemone-flowered variety, flowers from late July through August. And then, if relieved of every faded flower and stem, it blossoms again lightly in September and October. The name of Snowbank is no exaggeration for this eighteen-inch single white which produces a wealth of four-inch blooms all through the summer with a shining August emphasis. Of the doubles, the Zinnia-flowered shasta is at its height in June although it continues to a degree all summer long. The two-foot Mount Shasta, a chrysanthemum-flowered type, blooms uninterrupted from June until frost. Therefore if you are selecting but one shasta or *Chrysanthemum maximum*, let it be Mount Shasta, "probably the best white-flowering herbaceous perennial to date." In the cutting garden I have found a fifteen-foot row of these various shastas one of the most productive sections there. With roses in rose satin-glass bowls, they are enchanting.

To the fore of the border *Stokesia* Blue Moon with charming five-inch lavender discs, appears consistently attractive through summer and autumn, its neat foliage always in good order. A fairly unfamiliar composita, this cornflower aster is one of the more worth while fifteen-inch growers and delightful with the later shastas. If annual asters are one of the flowers which do not reciprocate your affection, this stokesia is a good substitute.

Where there is plenty of space and strong, robust, flashing subjects are suitable, there are three transition daisies which carry summer brilliance into autumn glory with no demand but staking. Helenium, Helianthus and Heliopsis are no toy plants to be tucked in an inconspicuous spot but deep, glowing subjects for mass plantings among shrubs, for backgrounds in very wide borders, for screens along garages or, as I use them, shields for the compost pits. Since any of the three attain some two feet of green growth early, they are well fitted to this use, nor does their rampant nature bother me for I transfer some of the double ring peony supports to them immediately the peonies are faded.

Helenium or Helen's flower comes in fine named varieties; all are grand to cut. I have particularly liked the gilt-edged dark mahogany Peregrina, three feet high and a mass of color in July and August, the lemon yellow, four-foot Riverton Beauty and the copper and gold Clippersfield Orange. These last two flower in August and September. Division for all of them is necessary in alternate years at least and preferably each spring.

Of the perennial sunflowers, *Helianthus multiflorus floraplena,* a clear yellow, four-foot variety, blooms from late summer into autumn and gives the effect of a small dahlia. It is a delectable plant.

As American as an Iroquois Indian is Heliopsis, the orange sunflower, which produces a molten glow of wiry-stemmed, daisy blooms from July into autumn. *H. scabra incomparabilis*, a three-foot variety rather double, won the Award of Merit in England in 1933 and is now gaining appreciation in this native land of the heliopsis.

All three of these summer into autumn growers need room so that it is wise to make their acquaintance with some diffidence. Start with a few plants of heleniums. You'll love bountiful summer baskets of them, for the porch or for deep window ledges in the sunroom.

Better known perhaps for late summer time are the rudbeckias or cone-flowers, especially such fine newer varieties as The King, with stiff-stemmed crimson flowers, and White Lustre, a dignified plant, bearing white-petaled blossoms with a metallic lustre to their prominent cones. The rudbeckias are also somewhat coarse-growing three-foot plants but most reliably hardy and tolerant of dryness and heat. They are just the perennials, in fact, for some sun-baked corner where the best of conditions do not prevail yet where space exists for increasing your cut flower supply.

Of distinguished hardy aster varieties there has long been a magnificent procession. Yet even among the most noteworthy kinds, *Aster frikarti*, Wonder of Staffa, which blooms from June until November, stands preëminent. Nurserymen consider it the "finest garden plant introduced during the past twenty years" while amateurs who make a practice of trying out some of each year's novelties consider *Aster frikarti* "marvelously satisfactory" and urge their friends to plant it freely. An enchanting lavender, this aster does well in light shade but in full sun it produces not just a fair showing of bloom but a rich, unfailing, long-season display. Plants average thirty inches high and flowers two and one-half inches across. They are superb for cutting. Among the taller hardy asters, the recently introduced pink Survivor is outstanding.

Finally—since such compositas as asters and chrysanthemums are included among the autumn flowers—I pass on now to the Transvaal daisy or gerbera. This tender perennial which is hardy south of Virginia and the florists' darling in the North, is, however, absolutely dependent here on cold frame wintering. But so elegant is its form and so enchanting its muted pastel tones, that more and more of us are finding this South African daisy essential for the cutting garden. From seed the gerbera is difficult. Germination is uncertain and it takes six to nine months of careful growing to obtain first flowers. But spring-purchased plants of the Jamesoni Giant Hybrids flower freely through the summer and may, I am told, continue as winter window-garden subjects if they are potted up in early September and moved indoors. I have not tried this but even if you discard them, as I do, at frost time I feel sure you will consider them worth your investment just for the narrow-petaled coral, gold, primrose and cream blossoms they have so constantly produced.

Every time I begin thinking over all the daisies I have grown, I get excited. Each one I've had I want to urge you to plant too. But what I really should suggest is that you find your way cautiously through this maze of composita varieties since the majority of them grow rapidly, produce abundantly and practically never die.

4. Daylilies for a Long Delight

DAYLILY is the pretty, common name given to two indispensable perennial families—hemerocallis and hosta. Both bear charming flowers of lily form. Both produce fine enduring foliage and are of easy culture. There resemblance ends since actually they are of most dissimilar appearance. Furthermore, in recent years the yellow or orange hemerocallis has received so much more of the hybridizers' attention than the white and lavender hosta that today it is hemerocallis alone which is usually known as daylily.

This perennial commends itself to us in many ways. In the border an early hemerocallis looks well as a strong sentinel placed through The Iris Strip. In the garden there is no better plant to face down shrubs or foundation evergreens, to use as colorful accent beside a flight of steps or to mass in a strong May to September succession of yellow, orange, gold and ruddier hues along a wide driveway or before a hedge.

If there is water, what lovelier accent can be found than a great fountainous clump of tall and delicate yellow lilies with pink mallows for background? If the gardener is flower-loving but pressed by many concerns, what better plant than the hemerocallis to give her colorful blooms outside or in? And for naturalizing, the daffodil finds a rival in drifts of daylilies set in the light dappled shade of trees.

These lilies are called flowers-of-a-day because in most varieties each blossom stays fresh for only one day, closing and fading at night. Recently, however, there have appeared a number like Patricia, Dauntless, Sovereign and Sonny which have open flowers in the evening. These you will want to include with your moonvines, flowering tobacco and white phlox if you dwell upon the scented evening beauty of your garden. The brief freshness of each blossom, however, does not preclude cutting. A stalk of hemerocallis, which in a variety like Sunny West or Golden West might carry fifty buds, stays fresh for a week indoors. Only you must each morning cut away the faded flowers of the day before. And bouquets rather than studied arrangements are the thing since the point of interest of daylilies shifts according to sequence of bloom on the flower stalk.

Culture is simple. Daylilies require little but space, at least two feet between plants, better another foot if you hope to have them unattended but uncrowded for three years. Then division and manuring of the soil maintains top-size blooms. Although average soil satisfies, this is a perennial which responds nicely to plenty of humus or manure. Furthermore, such an organically rich soil is moisture retentive and daylilies require this condition since they are not particularly drought-resistant. At least I have not found them so, although the claim is often made that they do well in a dry soil.

Full sun or light shade, either is suitable, but it is a mistake to expect any kind of flowering in dense shade. A good plan is to plant early-blooming varieties in full sunshine. This means color sooner than on plants of the same variety in the shadows. Set the later varieties where depth of color will not be weakened by searing summer sun.

Staking, even for the very tall background varieties like Hankow and Serenade, is unnecessary. Nor do these self-reliant, pest- and disease-resistant daylilies exact spraying. In fact, deep summer soakings during rainless weeks are practically their only requirement.

I think one of the most attractive plantings of hemerocallis I ever saw was in a friend's garden where near a little stream he planted divisions from my Hyperion clumps. In open shade there they grew to great stature, opening in July and August an abundance of flaring yellow blooms of fine texture, strength and quantity. The rosy Charmaine or gilded Dauntless also add distinction to the line of a small pool. In fact, this plant of recurving foliage crowned with delicate lily-form flowers belongs near any sort of water, pond, brook or pool, large or small.

The blooming season is long, extending from the fragrant May flowering lemon lily species to the multiflora hybrids in September. And almost every variety offered has quality. Considering that the greatest hybridizer of hemerocallis, Dr. A. B. Stout, has spent thirty years on this plant and has grown one hundred thousand varieties from which he has selected less than one hundred, this is understandable. Once our gardens held only the delicate short-season *H. flava* and the coarse tawny roadside *fulva*. Now we grow as many as we can accommodate and our interest is constantly stimulated by new varieties of definitely pink or red hues. Of these the thirty-six-inch *H. fulva rosea* is now the nearest to a pure pink. A clear white is also a future probability.

Select hemerocallis according to the season you need it and the color and height you prefer. In the border you will get a fine effect from one or two varieties spaced at long regular intervals—Apricot, for instance, to accompany iris days, the starry pink to yellow Serenade with belladonna or Summer Skies delphinium and Hyperion among the midseason phlox.

For close delight in summer plant the fragrant, lemon-yellow Patricia, which stays open through June and July evenings, the mahogany-marked Mikado and the tall and effective Sunny West with its attractive flaring flowers. I happen to like, too, the four-foot coppery *kwanso virginica* which faces down our blue hydrangeas by the porch and combines nicely with them in bouquets for the dim blue-papered hallway. This kwanso stays in flower from July to late August and is pleasing with such perennial blues as *Salvia farinacea* and *Aconitum sparksi.*

If you want later lilies, the small-flowering multiflora species, thirty inches high and orange, carries on through August and September. This is a floriferous rather than a distinguished hemerocallis. I like it, however, and its colorful hybrids too, to edge a distant, lightly-shaded shrubbery planting, the curving edge of which it thus brightly delineates from a distant view.

In case at this point you feel overwhelmed by these many daylily possibilities just go over the selected list of varieties on the chart. Six of these—Mikado, Hyperion, Patricia, Bagdad, Rajah and Ophir—came out with unassailable reputations when out of one hundred twenty-four varieties they were tested a few years ago by forty persons. You can grow the species like the sweet *flava*

Hemerocallis in Bright Succession

Variety	Color	Height in Inches	Season	Remarks
Apricot	True apricot	24	May	Medium-size flowers
Sovereign	Orange yellow	30		Day and evening flowers
Tangerine	Clear orange	20		Carries into June
Bagdad	Reddish orange	42	June into July	Prominent midrib, 5″ flower
Mikado	Orange	36		Eyed type with mahogany spots
Patricia	Pale yellow	30		Fragrant, also open at night
Serenade	Pink to yellow	48		Twisted, crinkled petals
Bijou	Red on orange	30	July	Many small flowers
Majestic	Orange	36		Evening also, ruffled 6″ flower
Cinnabar	Orange cinnamon	30	July and August	Medium size, long season
Hyperion	Canary yellow	40		Fragrant, 6″, handsome
Ophir	Golden yellow	54		Large and long flowering
Rajah	Dark orange to garnet	40		Prominent eye zone
Sunny West	Canary yellow	48		Very large flower, stems branching
Hankow	Yellow orange	42	September	Scarlet marking, 5½″ flower
Boutonniere	Yellow and peach	36		Small, attractive

from seed but for the hybrids buy divisions and these sparingly. A few daylilies in a very few years, you will find, cover a great deal of space nicely though, so you'll never regret your purchase.

Hostas

Perhaps it is because they are so utterly undemanding that my great favorites, the hostas or funkias, also of lily form, have been so completely unsung. Certainly their lack of acclaim is not my fault since I weary my fellow gardeners with their praises. But so completely charming is the white and fragrant August or Corfu lily and the small, pale *minor alba* in my garden that I cannot bear to see them neglected. And for arrangements, especially in clear green glass, they are the coolest-looking hot weather flower I know.

Is there indeed a plant which combines more attractive attributes with a practically self-supporting nature than the hosta? Prepare the soil rich and deep to begin with and assure moisture by locating near a stream or by deep summer soakings and what do you get? First a plant of handsome heart or lance-shaped foliage, pleasing from the time the early green spears appear in spring until in late October growth is checked by frost. Then a strong-stemmed flower of white or lavender, sometimes scented, and pretty enough, indeed, to have right beside the porch all summer long. Even a place in the sun is not required since the hostas all prefer light shade. And finally no pest or disease will appear and not a stake be required.

For many years I have enjoyed a bed of the August lily along the south side of our wisteria-hung veranda. The young leaves first appear with a setting of purple and yellow pansies before and tall yellow tulips behind them. As the hosta foliage develops the heat-ridden pansies are discarded but not replaced, since the growing perennials readily cover their retreat. Meanwhile self-sowing nicotiana seedlings from the border are placed among the tulips. Thus in summer nicotiana and hosta flower in fragrant unison and where the house forms the fourth side of a garden this three-foot bed is consistently colorful. You too may prefer by your porch such a flower bed rather than a typical all green "foundation planting." Futhermore, I commend to you a summer evening scented by Corfu lily and nicotiana.

I believe this *H. subcordata grandiflora* is the finest hosta of which I find fourteen varieties offered by one firm. I have these growing in my trial garden and consider that at least eight of them have particular merit and beauty. I even include *H. fortunei viridis marginata*, with its two-tone leaf, although variegated foliage is one of my prejudices. If you have lightly shaded areas which have proved difficult, if you need plants for naturalizing so as to reduce upkeep, if you have struggled over an angle by the cellar door or the kitchen steps or a narrow northern walk which presents one long plea for weeding, try there one of the hardy hostas.

There is a twelve-inch white, *H. minor alba*, which will make a nice edging in the shade. *H. sieboldiana*, eighteen inches, is an imposing silvery-foliaged specimen plant for

July. The two-foot *glauca* produces midsummer lavender bells, while *caerulea* is bluest and tallest of all and especially agreeable with a yellow hemerocallis like Sunny West. Narrow or heart-shaped foliage offers further variation in this extremely reliable plant group.

CHAPTER IX

IMPORTANT PERENNIALS FOR AUTUMN

1. Asters, Aconites and Anemones Herald the Season

As SUMMER wanes, the garden reaches a final peak of beauty. With hazy drifts of color in the sun, the Michaelmas daisies achieve a rich fruition, while in light shade, cool nights perfect the blue flames of aconites and the delicate pastel tints of anemones. Now with the heat of the season past, a new freshness comes both to the garden and to us as we linger among our flowers through the last delectable Indian Summer days.

Three types of hardy asters or Michaelmas daisies are valuable. Those really dwarf varieties, like the six-inch Lavanda and Niobe, make very nice edging plants if you prefer recurrent bloom at your border's rim instead of spring concentration there. Since aster foliage is good, you can achieve a pleasant sequence by alternating one-color masses of asters with plantings of May pinks or *nepeta* or both or, if you like autumn emphasis alone, you can achieve unusual September and October color with a completely fresh outline for your garden. These same varieties with a pink aster like Countess of Dudley are also attractive in front of shrubbery.

Through the center of the border plants of hardy asters of the *novi-belgi* or New York type look well. These grow from two and one-half to five feet so you will select for mid-section use only moderately tall varieties like the purple Amethyst, rosy Beechwood Challenger, White Mt. Everest or crimson Red Rover. For the rear of the garden or in luxurious masses before shrubbery, nothing is handsomer than the taller four- to five-foot light Blue Gown, deeper Gay Border Blue or silvery mauve Hilda Ballard with a pink like Sunset in between.

Mid-border asters prove more tractable if only three stems are allowed to develop on each plant. These are staked with inconspicuous bamboo. Nice cloudy growth then results without too much space consumption for each plant. If these New York asters are planted next oriental poppies, however, one extra side stem is allowed each plant and these side sprouts are pinched back a few inches early in July so that a shorter, bushier spray is available to fill in during the time when the poppy no longer has height.

For the rear of the border the *novae-angliae* or New England asters are autumn indispensables. I also value them as early green backgrounds for beds which have to be free standing and so lack an important backdrop of evergreen or flowering shrub. Their flowering then is but an additional blessing. Let this type have four stems to a plant. These though stiff must still be staked. Pinching off six inches of growth in July results in more grace but in less height, of course, so in shaping your plants be guided by purpose. In this group the new pink Survivor or Barr's pink and white Mt. Rainier make a charming background combination.

Good companions for Michaelmas daisies in September are the early chrysanthemums. The white Climax is charming with a single pink chrysanthemum like Astrid or Winsome. Since chrysanthemums lack blues, however, you may prefer these tones, especially the deep rich aster Violetta, to go among them. The lavender variety Queen Mary is also pleasing with such a lingering pale pink phlox as Mme. Paul Dutrie. And when you grow easy-from-seed dahlias of the Coltness hybrid strain, plant these with hardy asters for background. You will like the strong contrast of bold, shining-foliaged dahlias with pale misty clouds of aster bloom. I like, too, the combination of marigold Yellow Supreme with any of the blue varieties.

Perhaps outside the border where space is no object, you have growing on a trellis, the brilliant fall-fruiting firethorn shrub, *Pyracantha*. If so, set the rampant mauve species *Aster tataricus* before it with plants of chrysanthemum Autumn Glory, near by. Then in sections where November 1 concludes the garden year, these three will wave a gay flamboyant farewell.

Hardy asters have three cultural requirements—full sun, adequate summer moisture and yearly spring division. If this late April going-over is omitted, plants are never so satisfactory the second year as the first. They may even decline and disappear. Therefore, discard the woody centers each spring and in a new location or in the same place with fresh soil, bone meal enriched, put in three rooted sprouts to form a clump. Avoid crowding—a tall aster wants a three-foot area—or mildew will appear. It may anyway. Then you must get busy with a sulphur dust.

In vases too you will enjoy these easily arranged Michaelmas daisies. For the mantel I fill urns of them in blending colors. They keep fresh for a week if only I remember to add extra water daily. If you are on the flower committee of your church, depend on these luxuriant autumn perennials for your Sundays. You will find that they are large and important enough to be effective instead of overwhelmed when they are used for altar adornment. Late daylilies and dahlias go well with them. Buy your first aster plants. A few will go far by the second year. Only the species will come true from seeds.

Aconites

The monkshood, so called for the shape of its blossom, adorns its long spikes with a multiple blue array. Plant it, however, only in areas of light shade since aconite fails in full sun. Its other preferences are for a protected location, a great deal of moisture and a soil rich in leaf mold or old manure.

Sparks variety is the best late summer aconite. It has deep blue turrets, five feet tall. These are charming contrasts to masses of salmon and white phlox and lavender mistflower, *Eupatorium coelestinum*, all of which are shade tolerant. The Salmon Beauty beebalm or Monarda is another attractive Sparks companion.

The first year don't be surprised, however, if all you enjoy from aconites is finely wrought foliage. Color will appear the next year when your plants feel more at home. Restlessness is not a characteristic of this family.

Fischeri, a dark blue monkshood, blooms in September and October. One of the hardiest, it grows but two to three feet tall and appears at a time when spike flowers of deepest blue are valuable. Latest and tallest is *wilsoni*, the violet monkshood, a six- to seven-foot mauve variety which gleams through the October mists. Try either with white *Anemone alba* against a yew hedge and you will achieve an autumn memory which will last the winter through.

Unfortunately aconites are not the easiest of perennials to raise. Too many gardeners, indeed, report they "used to have aconites but they seem to have disappeared." Drought for one thing affects them most adversely, often causing leaves to blacken and curl and stalk by stalk to turn brown and collapse. Then, of course, no flowers appear. If this happens to A. *wilsoni* which you have awaited clear into October, it is a far from happy circumstance. Drought thus makes aconites appear diseased. Before you lift and burn and renew the soil of plants so affected—as you must do if it is verticillium wilt which has attacked your aconites—consider the season and the possibility that dryness alone has caused the trouble. Usually the diseased plant reveals a progressive dying upward of leaves while the dried-out plant browns all over.

Crown rot, mildew and poisonous roots, which must be handled carefully, are other aconite debits.

Considering all this, I still urge upon you the acquaintance of the aconites. If you soak them well in dry spells, maphap no ailments will develop. Certainly aconites are desirable if healthy, well-grown plants are at all possible.

Anemones

The Japanese anemones bring to the rich season of autumn the delicate tints of spring. From September until killing frosts they offer their white and rose sequence of waxen blooms, lovely for garden or house. *Alba* is the single, Whirlwind the old-fashioned double white, now superseded by Marie Manchard. September Charm is a silvery pink. Alice has lilac tones in its pink, and Queen Charlotte is a rosy semi-double. Prince Henry is of deeper tone, an early double crimson and lower growing than the others.

Be patient with anemones in their early days and they will reward you with a bright future. When they arrive late in spring, plant them in sun or light shade and in a spot where there is protection from wind but still a good circulation of air. It is fine if a wall or shrubbery border can protect them from the north while the plants themselves face south. The site must also be well drained and the soil richly and deeply prepared.

Anemones are, indeed, no casual sojourners in your garden. Therefore place them judiously and let them become well established until each plant has the root power to bear a great mass of flowers. In summer, cool the root runs with a mulch and be indefatigable about watering. In winter, cover the plants well with leaves.

Time will suggest many charming companions for these fall perennials which come into flower while many annuals are still at their height and the hardy asters and chrysanthemums are also staging their show. Aster Blue Gown, anemone Marie Manchard, and salmon zinnias are a lovely trio or against an evergreen background you may prefer aster Red Rover, *Aconitum fischeri* and *Anemone alba*. The mistflower is another good companion for anemones and also the tall daisy-decked *Boltonia asteroides*.

If, however, you share the opinion that for sheer loveliness of blossom, no other flower equals this one you may prefer to plant your anemones by themselves. Perhaps along a gray ivy-covered wall you will colonize Whirlwind or dwell upon September Charm as it justifies its name before the feathery green of hemlock. Alone or with companions, it will not matter; once anemones are established they inevitably become your autumn delight.

2. Chrysanthemums Dare the Garden to Die

LONG after the anemone and aconite have said farewell, long after we have put away summer's chintz and started the heater fires, chrysanthemums challenge winter with late and lavish blooms. Indeed, in some favorable seasons these perennials, which come into final flower at a time when nature seems most hostile to the garden, carry on even into December and in the very teeth of frost present fresh, crisp and beauteous blossoms.

These last beauties terminate a procession which begins late in August and reaches its height in October. Through these months chrysanthemums appear in many forms and a multitude of colors. At present you may select them from some five major classifications. Soon there may be further diversity since development among these perennials is still going forward rapidly. Especially are there signs of increased earliness. This does not interest me, however, since my concern is not with varieties which appear when asters and dahlias are still at their height. At that time chrysanthemums have garden rivals. I prefer them when they stand alone.

Consider first the dwarf Cushion 'mums. Compact growing, one foot high and two feet wide, such kinds as Queen and Champion Cushion and Bronze Gold flower freely from September, or even a bit sooner, for many weeks into the fall. The lower Cushions are a good landscape type to use as edging for a very wide perennial bed, as outline for a shrubbery border or along driveway or walk.

The Rubellum hybrids of which Clara Curtis is typical are also low and bushy and usually in pink shades. They are not such compact growers and seem to me more attractive with their airier manner of growth.

The Koreans are tall, rather loosely formed plants with handsome, mainly October flowers in both single and double varieties. Of these there is a multitude including Vesta, Crimson Splendor, Lavender Lady, Red Velvet,

King Midas and Mrs. Pierre S. du Pont, every one of which is a beauty.

Somewhat later the buds of the daisy-like *arcticum* hybrids or Northland Daisies open. Kristina and Siegfried are in this class and also a group known as de Petris Hybrids. These to date do not include large doubles but I prize them highly for disease-resistant foliage and complete winter hardiness.

Finally there are the much diversified Pompons, small and large, early and late with varieties for every week in the long and lovely chrysanthemum season. Jewel, Judith Anderson, Irene, Little Bob and Pigmy Gold are button types. Eugene A. Wander, Jean Treadway, Granny Scoville are very handsome, large doubles.

To begin with consider this group of twelve which I think of as a good All-Season, All-Color Dozen—baker's! It includes favorites of mine which for one reason or another have received many good marks in my chrysanthemum note book. Later, your own experience and taste will indicate the perfect dozen for you, or very likely many more. But for a start you will enjoy White Cloud and Avalanche and in shades of pink, rose and lavender, Winsome, Jean Treadway and Lavender Lady, in yellow and bronze tones, Yellow Spoon, King Midas, Eugene A. Wander and Mrs. Pierre S. du Pont III (peach) with the deeper Crimson Splendor, Red Velvet, Rapture and The Chief added for contrast.

I prefer to grow chrysanthemums either in cutting rows among the vegetables or in separate beds featuring either whites and pastels to burgundies or else pale and deep yellows, bronze reds and a few pale blends like Coral Sea. A friend of mine who has the handsomest chrysanthemum border I know, over a period of four years has selected and associated plants which on a bright October day always lead me to ask, "Is there a sunset missing?" Her border (see plan on page 141) with its background of shrubs grows on a little slope to the south of the house, and is particularly beautiful looked down on from the dining-room window.

I have richly tinted chrysanthemums running along my hawthorne hedge since I do not include them in my mixed hardy border. Unless a bed is wider than my eight-foot allowance, it seems to me chrysanthemums take up too much spring and summer space there without offering color. Furthermore, when in October my favorites do flower, there is a very tired end-of-season look to the borders and few desirable companions for these late perennials. Therefore I prefer to feature chrysanthemums separately.

But it's easy enough to grow them through the summer in a place of their own and then to move them, on a cloudy September day when they are in bud, to the border. There space is easily made by pulling out some of the weariest annuals. If roots are well soaked before and after moving, the chrysanthemums bloom on without missing a beat. For early Korean or de Petris varieties this is a particularly good plan since these start flowering before mid-October.

If you want chrysanthemums for late fall cutting and cherish hopes of early December bouquets, plant in as

Border Unit of Chrysanthemums in Rich Autumn Shades
Hemlock Hedge or Shrubbery Background ~ 6'x20'

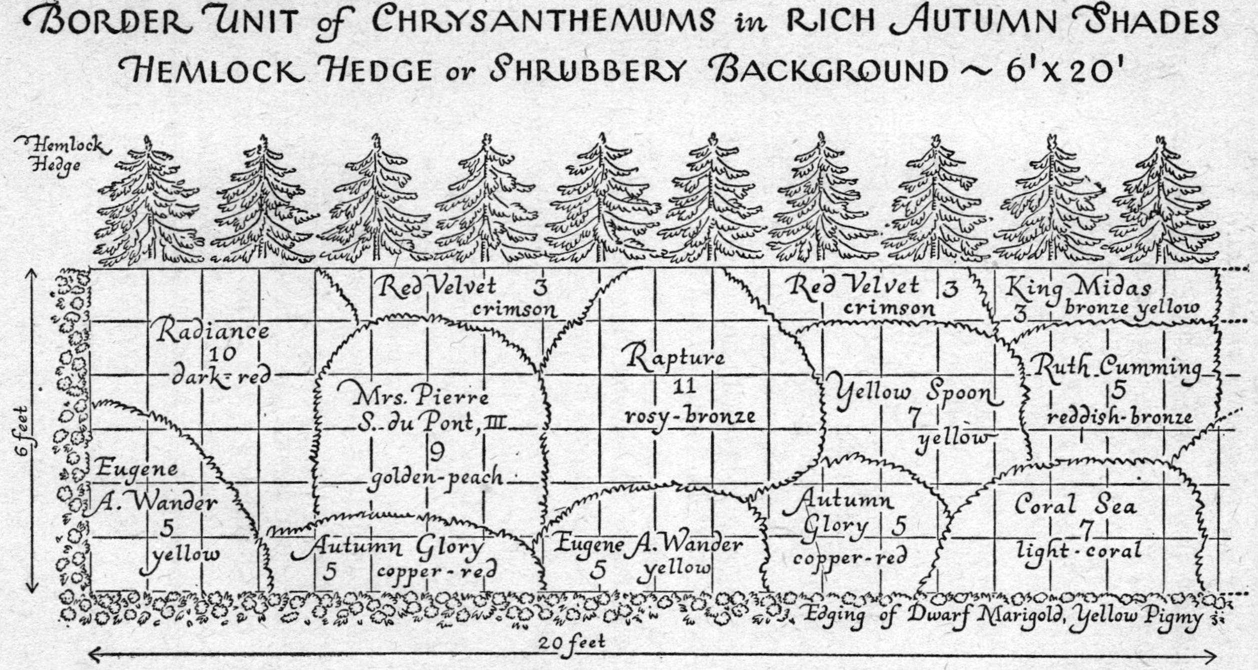

Scale ~ 1 square = 1'

Numbers in sections = number of plants required.

protected a spot as you have such de Petris varieties as Radiance, Autumn Glory and Coral Sea. These sometimes continue to flower until the first week of the last month in the year. If autumn has its droughty spells, be sure to water them to keep up their spirits for this important late season role.

Location is an important factor, of course, for all plantings. It should be protected where winds will not rock the plants about or a cooking, early morning sun destroy tissues sometimes frozen the night before. I notice that if flowers can recover slowly, not suddenly from severe cold, their endurance is remarkable. Undoubtedly a southwestern exposure is best with house wall, fence or shrubbery behind the planting for a windbreak.

Good drainage is essential, particularly in its relation to winter hardiness. Plants which are alternately ice-locked and thawed rarely survive an average open winter. Plants on a little slope covered, after the first crusty freeze, with salt hay or oak leaves held in place by boards or the more sightly evergreen boughs, pass the safest outdoor winters.

If even under such conditions your chrysanthemums have proved poor survivors, either treat them as indispensable annuals to be purchased every spring or take up a plant of each variety you cherish and afford it safe wintering in the cold frame. This is the method. After plants have flowered and well before a hard freeze, cut back the tall tops to crown growth. Soak the roots well and transfer the plants to the cold frame. Water again after planting and each week thereafter until a hard freeze occurs. The idea is to encourage as much rooting as possible in the new location. Then cover lightly with oak or other hardwood leaves or salt hay and fasten down the glass of the frame. To avoid overheating by the sun, cover the glass. If you have a lath screen used for summer shading, lay this on top.

From January on as warm middays occur, prop the glass up for short periods of ventilation. When in March examination reveals green growth, remove the leaf covering and the cold frame shade. By the first of April you can usually let the glass stay up all day and, as weather permits, at night too. This hardens plants so they can face open conditions again. Separate and transfer your chrysanthemums back to the garden when new growth is a few inches high. This is a fairly arduous business but the only sure way I have found to hold over certain exquisite but often tender favorites like the spoons, Eugene A. Wander, Granny Scoville and other favorites.

Investigate also the various de Petris hybrids. These are so hardy they are wintered without any covering. I have, in fact, not lost one and their crowns are persistently green all winter long.

Chrysanthemum beds need be prepared but ten inches deep unless natural drainage is poor. Then an extra six inches is dug and a layer of cinders or broken bricks laid in the bottom. This leads off water which otherwise would linger dangerously around the roots and be a real hazard to safe wintering.

If new beds are prepared in autumn, there is plenty of time for settling before spring planting. This is in May for new plants from the grower's but mid-April for home wintered stock which is at that time regularly separated (except for the Cushions which are divided every second year) into as many small rooted divisions as the outside of each crown will supply. Discard the hard woody centers. Then set the divisions out twelve to eighteen inches apart depending upon the nature of their mature size. Autumn Glory, for instance, needs but a square foot to a plant while Red Velvet and King Midas take much more. Plenty of room and a free circulation of air are essential for both looks and health.

Average cultivated garden soil grows very nice chrysanthemums but the bed made fertile with manure, humus or compost and later enriched with additional plant food, produces very fine flowers indeed. For extra feedings I use a dried manure product or some balanced plant food. Either is scattered in a ring under the outermost leaf spread of the established plant about the middle of June and again the first and middle of July. It is immediately watered in.

When after the spring resetting, your plants have six leaves, pinch the tops out to induce side branching and a type of growth to minimize staking. As each new branch develops six leaves, pinch these too. Discontinue this practice by mid-July for early varieties like Avalanche and Mme. Chiang Kai-shek. Continue until August for later flowering ones. Let growth go on then or flower formation may be fatally delayed. Be guided also by the time of first frost in your locality. In periods of prolonged drought, usually about three times a season, water chrysanthemums deeply with a Soil Soaker or by placing a slow running hose on a board for at least an hour in each area of the bed.

As a routine matter, and before pests appear, dust plants regularly with nicotine or rotenone until buds begin to open. If only de Petris varieties are grown, however, it may be possible to avoid dusting altogether, anyway until aphids actually are evident.

Staking for the taller Koreans seems inevitable. Separate bamboo or wire stakes fastened to each main stem by a 'twistem look well or you may set three stakes around each plant and encircle it with a piece of green twine or raffia. I have seen in certain public gardens, however, a quite adequate supporting job done by thrusting strong, much branched pieces of brush among the plants just as we have long done in the vegetable garden for peas. Cushions and Rubellums, of course, need no such attention.

As for the practice of disbudding, single varieties are more charming in great undisbudded sprays though large-flowering types like Winsome or Burgundy will produce even finer blooms if you remove some of the side buds from each cluster. Large-flowering doubles like Mrs. Pierre S. du Pont, Lavender Lady, and Granny Scoville could be disbudded to advantage. But in the garden where mass loveliness rather than greenhouse individuality is desirable, few of us enthusiasts find disbudding worth while.

If there is a complaint against chrysanthemums—and I hesitate to admit one since these are my most cherished perennials and this my favorite chapter—it is that in some seasons and for some varieties an unattractive browning of the lower foliage occurs. This may be due to the effect on plant tissues of drought followed by wet spells or it may be the result of a nematode attack. Selection of resistant varieties like White Cloud, Winsome, Coral Sea, Burgundy, Mrs. du Pont, Sequoia, Warrior, Red Velvet and Eugene A. Wander, which have been bred away from this tendency, attention to deep watering in times of drought and application of a deterrent dust will minimize or even eradicate this trouble.

Chrysanthemums You Must Not Miss!

SINGLES

WHITE
- North Star (early)
- White Spoon

BRONZE TO COPPER
- Autumn Lights (semi-double)
- Jasper Spoon
- Saladin

PINK
- Pink Spoon
- Winsome

RED
- Crimson Splendor
- The Chief (gold-tipped, semi-double)

LAVENDER TO PURPLE
- Dubonnet
- Orchid Spoon

YELLOW
- Arctic Queen
- Yellow Spoon

DOUBLES

WHITE
- Avalanche (early)
- Jean Cumming
- White Cloud (early)

BRONZE TO COPPER
- Ember (late)
- Granny Scoville
- Indian Summer (late)
- Mme. Chiang Kai-shek (early)
- Mrs. Pierre S. du Pont, III (peach)
- Rapture

PINK
- Jean Treadway (early)
- Rose Glow (early)

RED
- Burgundy
- Red Velvet
- Ruby Pompon
- Warrior (late)

LAVENDER TO PURPLE
- Burgundy
- Lavender Lady
- Symphony (mauve)

YELLOW
- Algonquin (early)
- Carrie
- Eugene A. Wander (early)
- King Midas
- R. Marion Hatton (early)
- Sequoia

In any case do grow chrysanthemums, selecting only the earlies if you live where the growing season is brief and frosts come soon, but September, October, and November varieties if your garden grows where so long a pageant is in most years possible. If you want chrysanthemums for cutting choose colors that suit the decoration of your house through the autumn months and be sure to include a few of the gerbera-like spoons. If you prefer the garden effect, I recommend these as charming color groupings—Arctic Queen, Rapture and Autumn Glory with Eugene A. Wander for foreground; Jean Treadway, Silver Moon and Lavender Lady with Coral Sea for edging; King Midas (this can be trained to form a little tree) Rapture, Mrs. Pierre S. du Pont III and Carrie with Autumn Glory for foreground, and the gold-tipped The Chief with any pure yellow like Algonquin. Finally here is a chart of my own favorites to use until your preference and experience dictate a more valuable one for your own garden.

CHAPTER X

IMPORTANT PERENNIALS FOR WINTER

1. Christmas and Lenten Roses Bloom in the Snow

When the firm hand of winter is laid upon our gardens, it seems impossible that a fresh crop of flowers should start blooming there. Yet where the Christmas rose is planted blossoms appear in December, since this hellebore scorns the sun and ease of summer and waits for the cold to flaunt unrivaled its white drifts of waxen bloom and bud. According to legend this is the rose which centuries ago bloomed on the first Christmas Eve. Now when temperatures are not far above zero, its flowering seems as miraculous today as it did centuries ago.

Yet this is a miracle which readily occurs since these perennials are culturally simple to deal with and once established, richly productive. No longer, indeed, is it necessary for chrysanthemums to have the last word when the Christmas roses fill each established clump with fat and numerous buds long before the late chrysanthemums are spent, while their close relatives, the

Lenten roses, are in fine flower before the spring crocuses show a trace of color.

If you are an enthusiast with a desire to make a hobby collection of these hellebores you can with determination and time locate a variety of them. One of the loveliest, *Helleborus niger*, the Christmas rose species, as well as the usual mixed varieties of *H. orientalis*, the Lenten rose, are readily available from many growers. *H. niger* grows eight to ten inches high with deeply serrated evergreen leaves and in time twenty to thirty flowers to a plant. These blossoms on sturdy stems, frequently in pairs, resemble the single-flowered tuberous-rooted begonias or some of the anemones. As the months go by the flowers pass from white through many beautiful rose-pink shadings and finally turn a pleasant enduring green.

When I cut them for bouquets I select both white and pink blooms and, in order not to sacrifice the important evergreen foliage, I select leaves from one of the aralia-like deciduous hellebores. For a special centerpiece Christmas roses with hemlock are unusual and exquisite, and the flowers stay fresh for three to four weeks. *H. altifolius* is the largest flowering of niger varieties. It grows twelve to sixteen inches high and produces flowers three to five inches across, often several on the same stem.

In the beginning it takes patience with these hellebores. Usually they do not flower either the first or even the second year after planting since they must, before setting buds, not only attain an unusual degree of maturity but also have made themselves completely at home. It is therefore important at the outset to select permanent quarters for them. One happily located group of fifteen niger plants, which my friend Isabel Fasel developed from one plant set out some thirteen years ago, opens each year well before Christmas some sixty flowers in a lively white to rose profusion. They make a surprising winter picture with an ancient oak tree spreading above them and the protecting wall of an old spring house for background.

In some years this planting, which is in West Chester, Pennsylvania, begins flowering by October 10 with new buds still opening at the New Year. Until late in March the blossoms, by that time green, linger on the plants. As a rule, however, bloom on *Helleborus niger* is not to be expected before November.

Near this planting grow also several varieties of *orientalis*, a species originally found in Asia Minor. The palmate foliage reaches twelve inches while the Lenten roses, so called because they always are present at Easter time although they start blooming much earlier, rise on twenty-inch stems. More than a hundred blossoms may appear on a well-established plant. *Orientalis* has exceedingly beautiful foliage which inclines to die down once very cold weather sets in in January. The color range of the flowers is from pale green through white, rose, claret and purple to light brown and a deep chocolate-red. Some varieties are maroon spotted. One, Irene Kroneman, is a rich brown, with leaves which tend to be evergreen. The very handsome flowers suggest certain cypripediums and are as charming as orchids for corsages.

Choice, lovely and hard to find is *H. foetidus*, a species

from western Europe. It produces a thick two-foot stem of slimly segmented leaves in the center of which develops a loose pale green globe of inflorescence. The flowers start slowly to open before Christmas, are perfected late in January and continue to look well for a month or so longer. Several stems spring from each crown in four- or five-year-old plants thus producing the effect of a small shrub, which is reminiscent somehow of *leucothoe* and just as attractive for the foreground of a shrubbery planting.

For an indoor arrangement *foetidus* is also a treasure. Late one January, I placed a single tall spray of it in a dull gold jar with a black Chinese base. The deep green of the foliage and the pale green of the flowers blended beautifully with the yellow and looked particularly well in with my eighteenth-century furnishings. And incidentally for an unusual flower show piece nothing could be more interesting than *H. foetidus* since it immediately commands attention and as a keeper is unexcelled. When after two weeks mine wilted, I revived it for another charming ten days by steeping the freshly cut stem for five minutes in a cup of boiling water and then plunging the spray again into its tall vase refilled with ice water.

Flowers on *H. foetidus* usually do not appear until early in December but in some particularly fortuitous seasons first color is seen a month ahead of schedule, in November. This species readily self-sows but seedlings do not bloom until the third year.

H. viridis from Hungary can sometimes be obtained but its smaller greenish flowers are attractive only to those who are collecting hellebores. It sometimes starts budding as early as December but the flowers do not open until March and the leaves are not evergreen. I have liked it for miniature arrangements. It too keeps fresh for weeks.

Elegant and unusual as these hellebores are, there is no great skill required in raising them. In your average garden soil they will do well enough but because of the permanency of their residence, it seems worth while to prepare an ideal plot of loam well mixed with leaf mold and sand until it feels coarse and light and is reliably moisture-retentive. A top dressing of leaf mold and rotted manure with slight yearly additions is always recommended for hellebores but you will find that an inch layer of composted material is an entirely satisfactory substitute. Mrs. Fasel's large planting has been grown without either manure or mulching but in leafy soil to which she has added bone meal each November.

Most important of all is location. A cool, moist, lightly shaded situation with protection from north and west winds which tend to burn foliage, seems best. The closer plants are to a protecting wall the earlier they will bloom. Their taste for shade makes these hellebores a special boon if you crave flowers but are frustrated by the deep shadows of trees. Beneath these in a fern bed or at the edge of shrubbery plantings, hellebores will do beautifully.

Set plants out at anytime from spring to October. August, however, will prove to be a particularly propitious time. New leaves appear in spring and when a plant has reached the six- or seven-leaf stage it is time to divide it. Otherwise the buds on *niger*, for example, come up so thickly they can hardly find space in which to open. Even in the first year of flowering there are six or seven blooms to a plant. In the course of a decade one *Helleborus niger* specimen will be capable of sufficient division to provide some thirty plants.

Niger does not produce seed in some localities, possibly because most of the flowers are fertilized just before extremely cold weather sets in and the seeds do not have a chance to develop. In the same place both *orientalis* and *foetidus* may seed freely. *H. foetidus* will produce quantities which ripen in June from flowers fertilized in February and March. All hellebore seed grows best when it is planted immediately after ripening. Seeds need cold weather, however, before germination is likely to take place. And signs of growth may not occur for two years. And then perhaps three more years may elapse before flowers appear. Obviously I can not recommend hellebores from seed to the impatient.

Through the summer your hellebores will change little. They seem simply to wait for autumn. Occasionally in times of prolonged drought the foliage wilts a little. Soak them deeply if this occurs. Otherwise even extra watering does not seem necessary for these most easy-to-grow perennials.

In fact, more trouble is often taken with the hellebores than is necessary. I see recommended the practice of lifting and forcing plants. Since despite cold and snow the hellebores bloom anyway, I can't see the point of forcing.

It is, indeed, part of the pleasure of growing hellebores that they afford us the special delights of inconsistency. In December, with one hand to reach for galoshes as snow protection and with the other for the picking basket and shears is for most of us a rare experience. Midsummer blooms grown in the open on midwinter plants—therein lies the charm of the hellebores.

Christmas Roses for Winter Cutting.

❧ ❧

CHAPTER XI

SECONDARY SPIRES

IN THE long border, especially if it can be seen from a distance, several spires other than delphinium are also rhythmically effective. The gardener who knows music finds that the repetition of the same flower form gives continuity to the whole as if the same chord were struck over and over again in a prelude. And, if she has a keen esthetic sense, she syncopates this primary rhythm with a secondary theme of lower spire flowers. For example, if the yellow thermopsis dominates June, blue lupines become perfect secondary steeples with white Lingard phlox the repeated chord.

Large groups of spires, however, are not placed together or the valuable pyramidal form of the individual is lost. Usually a single developed plant of any of these flowers considered spire-like suffices. A well-grown Chimney bellflower, for instance, will send up from a single crown several purple or white rockets while others of the steepled clan are often even more prolific.

The background of the spire should be unassuming. A flowering shrub or brilliantly berried bush may vie with the turrets of garden flowers and so rob them of the restful beauty. A plain wall of hemlock darkness, the quiet green of euonymus, the soft rose red of a brick wall, the gleam of a white picket fence, or the peaceful blue of sky or sea are ideal backgrounds.

In selecting our primary spire flowers for the various seasons we must require definite qualities. Obviously the predominant characteristic must be height, not usually less than five feet, and the blossom of steepled form preferably with the leaves growing in a low crown so that a long line of stem is visible. Plants must be moderately sturdy too, never even artistically loose in the manner of the carefree hardy aster. Their night value, for the garden, sought at twilight, is also worth considering.

Spires of Spring

The spires of spring are slow to appear for it takes a long stretch of growing weather to perfect a five-foot flower spike. Perhaps for the sake of an early show, and that not until June, it is wise to lower the standard and admit for this season a four-foot beauty, *Digitalis Isabellina,* a pale moonlit yellow. This is one of the loveliest of the foxgloves, and fine for our purpose because of its definite, sturdy form. Also unlike most foxgloves, Isabellina is perennial.

Foxgloves give strength and dignity to any border planting and "consort well with nearly every other flower, and certainly with every other color." The biennial Giant Shirley Hybrids, reaching a four- to six-foot height, are articularly fine in their wide range of color from white and shell pink to deep rose. For Isabellina a foreground planting of pink columbines is attractive with masses of lavender *Nepeta mussini* in front of these.

And for late spring the beautiful *Thermopsis caroliniana* is also not to be overlooked. How rarely I see this in gardens, although it is easily grown in the sun and choice for cutting. Indeed, where delphiniums are too difficult, this five-foot yellow thermopsis is a charming steepled substitute, and it is readily developed from seed too, if this is sown in early spring while the soil is still cool. Age increases its stature as it does with children, the third year thermopsis being mature while the second-year plants are only twenty-four-inch infants.

There are two choice secondary spires for this season of similar form and both blue—lupine and baptisia or wild indigo. I do not include the strain of Russel lupines. These, of course, grow taller and produce a wide color range but since they do not care for my garden or thrive in any of my friends' plots either, I am not well acquainted with them. Evidently even the selected American seed is still dependent on the cool humidity its English ancestors enjoyed. Of these the remark seems true, "the weather that grows corn, kills the lupine."

The more reliable *Lupinus polyphyllus* and its pink and white relatives develop two- to three-foot spikes of enchanting blooms in June. These rise from finely-cut, soft gray-green leaves. White lupines are particularly lovely grown with the pink oriental poppy Helen Elizabeth, and blue masses of Chinese delphinium which detract from their usual summer retreat. After lupines fade, cut the stalks low and let the plants rest for several weeks. Then water them deeply and feed them to encourage a September crop. If they disappear for a time, keep the space for them open and marked. Do not interplant.

Since our hot, dry summers are not at all to the lovely lupine's liking, it is essential for their survival that the conditions we can control be ideal. A well-drained site in full sun but with protection from wind is good. There prepare a light, moisture-retentive rich soil. I always add plenty of sand to the lupine bed too and in the spring work a dried cow manure product among the plants. During their growing season and after their midsummer rest, an abundance of moisture is essential. Transplantings are best managed in autumn.

Baptisia australis is a pet of mine. It is three feet high, deep blue and lupine-like but easier to grow, and with a large generous plant form reliably handsome the entire growing season. This makes it fine for important placement in a sizeable border even though its blooming season lasts but a few May or June weeks. If you are not acquainted with baptisia, do seek it out. It is a lovely thing especially for busy gardeners who want continuously attractive borders on a minimum attention schedule. Buy a few plants to start with. Then increase your stock, as you will certainly want to, by sowing your own freshly gathered seed in a cold frame in midsummer. There it will germinate, though probably not until the next spring.

Summer Verticals

Summer spires are more numerous than those of spring. In June and July the lovely *Astilbe*, Salland, reaches its peak of perfection. The distinctive yucca, too long disgraced by unskillful planting, shakes out its bells in June. The chimney bellflowers appear in July when "flaunts the flaring hollyhock" as well.

When the background is a white fence or brick wall, hollyhocks are the inevitable choice. They are most effective, as Gertrude Jekyll has pointed out, if the wall is not too high and the spires shoot up "telling well against the distant tree masses above the wall." They are particularly effective too if the garden slopes down a hill and their varying heights outline the declivity. I saw them thus, both singles and doubles, in all the pink shades with Dorothy Perkins roses strewn over the wire fence behind them and larkspur and ragged robins complementing their hues. A mulberry tree in the background emphasized the cheerful uprightness of the hollyhocks.

Yucca has long had the unhappy fate of growing singly and centrally in front yards of unhappy visage. Used with some relation to its surroundings it displays an unusual and individual beauty, its "tall columns like shafts of marble against the hedge trees. In the daytime the yucca's blossoms hang in scentless, greenish white bells, but at night these bells lift up their heads and expand with great stars of light and odor—a glorious plant. Around their spires of luminous bells circle pale night moths lured by the rich fragrance." Yucca can be counted on to emphasize the framework of a design. It is unexpectedly fine too as an individual accent plant in each corner of a small formal garden.

For midsummer, *Cimicifuga racemosa,* snakeroot, is a lovely spire suited to a shady place. Each spike is covered with feathery white blossoms. Let the tall white *Clematis erecta,* the lower white *Veronica spicata alba* and blue *Clematis integrifolia caerulea* stand near *Cimicifuga racemosa.*

Campanula pyramidalis is one of my favorite steeples for strong summer effect. It is either purple or white with star-shaped blossoms. This chimney bellflower, although often perennial, is not reliably hardy in some sections and is often, like most of the foxgloves, therefore, best renewed every year. Purple and white hostas and the tall heat-loving betony contrast pleasantly with this bellflower. Where a border is free standing and lacks shrub or wall background, this bellflower and the taller delphinium interplanted maintain a fairly constant rear guard.

For secondary points in summer, selection can be made from the Japanese astilbes. These are the feathery branching flowers the florist forces at Easter time, gift plants of which can be set out permanently in the border. With my passion for fine plant form, I am keen on astilbes of all kinds. In a shaded section of my border, I have a colony of *Astilbe,* Peach Blossom, a pale pink variety which earns a special blessing every June. Deliciously fragrant, we all enjoy it on the table, while a plant which in five years has required absolutely nothing of me beyond yearly fertilizing and a few summer soakings is one to elicit paeons of praise.

Some time when you are weary of the vagaries of columbine or the infections of delphinium, plant a lot of astilbes and enjoy a few seasons of utter peace. Varieties to consider for foreground are the white Deutschland, pink Peach Blossom, garnet Fanal and salmon Granat. Usually the pastel pinks are fairly tepid, a fact I don't mind, however.

The gas plant, *Dictamnus fraxinella*, is another undemanding gem. With an eye to permanence select for it a sunny location in deep, rich loam. When it thus has its way, it lives and thrives in the same spot for generations. Slow to establish, it eventually grows to thirty inches and raises from the midst of fine, ash-like foliage a rose or white turret of exquisite form and color. This is a foreground spire of undeniable worth to all who wish to garden for the future as well as the present. Here is plant quality of the finest kind. Space dictamnus at five- or eight-foot intervals just behind the edging of a border and let its companion be blue flax. You will then have added a note of real distinction to the planting.

I enjoy, too, the lemon odor of the foliage and the fun of seeing the flowers flash when touched with a lighted match. Because of the volatile oil emitted as a vapor from these, the dictamnus is commonly called burning bush or gas plant. It is grown from seed sown an inch deep in the open as soon as it is ripe. The next spring sprouts show but not until the third year are flowers likely to begin appearing. For an unusual arrangement, dictamnus also has fine possibilities.

Likewise good to cut and of long season border value are the veronicas or speedwells. These produce fine stalwart foreground spires of purple, rose or white for July, August and September. They are easily propagated by seed or division and a constant joy because of good foliage and easy culture.

It is important, however, to select veronicas with care and under no circumstances to take in gift plants whose habits are not known to you. *Veronica longifolia* is a weedy grower you will be likely to wish you had never met, but *Veronica longifolia subsessilis* is one of the best, two feet tall, with continuously good foliage and showy deep purple spikes through midsummer. Blue Spires is a worth-while improved spicata for early summer effect and noteworthy for heat- and drought-resistance.

Autumn Turrets

For early fall, I like the well-named gayfeathers. *Liatris scariosa*, September Glory, lifts a fine strong purple cone some five feet tall. White Spire is a beauty too, and a better choice if red, orange or purple abounds in the border, since September Glory clashes with most rich warm shades.

Finally for late autumn there are the shade-loving aconites, marvelous when they thrive, which could be more often. Plant them in that section of the border which passes under a tree. There they will rise like dark blue torches.

These spire flowers are a fascinating group but not all of them, of course, would be right in any one garden. Their value both outdoors and in bouquets lies essentially in the contrasts they afford. Plant them therefore near loose, massive material and in arrangements note how interesting they are when combined with the globes of daisies or the mists of gypsophila. Purple veronicas with white shastas, for example, make a charming, clean-cut appearance while blue baptisia contrasts effectively with the golden gaillardia Mr. Sherbrook. And in the shrubbery border too, especially when it is in an all-green summer stage, the ivory spires of yucca are a splendid sight.

CHAPTER XII

GRACE NOTES FOR THE GARDEN

VARIETY is the spice of gardens too. When borders are exclusively planted with masses of lance-leaved iris, grassy daylilies and globular phlox, they inevitably lack grace. It takes the lilting sprays of columbine, flax and coralbell, or the gossamer clouds of gypsophila and sea lavender skillfully interplanted with these heavier subjects to produce that air of delicacy and charm which makes a garden an enchanted spot.

Yet who would seek a reason beyond their own attractiveness to plant columbines? Captivating in their own right, those poised butterfly blossoms are a delight for garden or vase. In May and June they flower just on the heels of the early tulips and since their heights—according to the species or variety—vary from low to medium, their place is in the foreground of the border just behind the edging plants.

If you are not acquainted with the columbines, or more properly, aquilegias, you can obtain a good survey picture by purchasing some fall or very early spring a plant each of such species as *A. chrysantha*, a thirty-inch yellow which is likely to go on flowering up to July; A. *caerulea*, the twenty-inch pale blue Rocky Mountain columbine; and the ten-inch white fan columbine, A. *flabellata nana alba*, with the best foliage of them all. Then obtain three plants of the eighteen-inch Scott Elliott hybrids and at least one of that choice newer variety, Crimson Star. Personally I would not lack a single one of these. You will find, however, that they are usually not very long-lived perennials though some may last into the third year. If this happens, you can increase your stock by dividing the crowns in September.

It is more likely, however, that you must keep your crop of columbines in hand by sowing seeds about every other June. The seeds will germinate slowly so keep the bed watered until actual green appears and don't stop a week short of success because you think your crop has failed. Allow the separated seedlings then to remain in the cold frame until spring, transplanting them as early as weather permits to their flowering positions in the border.

A packet of Wayside Giant Pinks or Giant Blues produces something pretty special, I assure you. For effective border contrast, try a colony of these in front of a blue iris like Shining Waters with the pale yellow meadowrue, *Thalictrum glaucum*, behind the iris. Use columbine freely between the Darwin tulip stretches and if your garden is tiny and every plant there must count for succession, precede the columbines with a dozen early tulips, among which you can scatter annual larkspur seed in September. Follow the columbines, then, with your favorite perennial phlox and a few chrysanthemum plants. Never a dull week will be the result of even such a limited procedure.

Species columbine seem to prefer a rather heavy, clay soil but for your hybrids you must prepare a sandy, humusy home. Both thrive either in full sun or light shade but are not drought-resistant and so need extra summer watering. I enjoy in the apple tree bed bleedinghearts with the fan and chrysantha columbines which have been reliably perennial there. I hope your plants will be spared leaf miner attack. Mine recovered from the labyrinthian tunnelings of these pests when I was constant about cutting off attacked foliage and dusted them several times with rotenone. If you are using a nicotine contact spray elsewhere for aphids, this will destroy the leaf miner too.

The feathery, true-blue linum or flax, also blooming in May or June, is another means of grace. Although there are also white and yellow varieties, they do not compare with the enchantment of the blue *Linum perenne*. Charming with white or yellow tulips, with iris and with white phlox Miss Lingard, this fifteen-inch plant is most pleasing for a foreground planting.

Select a sunny spot and supply a well-enriched sandy soil or you will find, as I once did, that its sojourn with you is much too brief. Its foliage is nothing but its azure shower of fine petals is as pretty on the plant as on the ground which it literally "blues" around it every June morning in my garden. By removing at the earth line the shoots which have flowered you can induce thicker growth and longer flowering. I couldn't say of *Linum perenne* that it is as indispensable as is peony or iris, only that you'll love it and treasure it for color and pleasant individuality.

The coralbells or heucheras enter the picture a few weeks later than linum, though for a time their pink and blue blooms can be delightfully concurrent. The heucheras produce twelve- to fifteen-inch airy racemes of rosy or white blooms from late May to July with some sporadic flowering even into autumn. The coral red variety, Pluie de Feu, and the pink Rosamundi are choice. Indeed, I know no prettier small plant. The crowns of finely-edged heart-shaped leaves with reddish tints never fail in beauty from spring till fall so that you can use heucheras prominently, even as edging, knowing they will always look well. Their delicate panicles are a particularly attractive contrast to intermediate iris or late tulips and for bouquets an adorable filler.

I have now a long line of Pluie de Feu beside a flagstone walk. Divisions every third year from the original six purchased plants produced these undeniable treasures but you can readily get a stand from seeds as well. I am told heucheras want sun but they have done well for me in light shade too. The soil, however, must be rich and, of course, well drained. A spring top dressing of well-decayed or dried manure seems to delight them and increase their flowering.

For tall early summer and lower late effect there is the gossamer babysbreath. Only a few plants of this are needed since in time each one covers almost a three-foot area. In each of my thirty-foot units beside the blue delphiniums I have two specimens of the double, choice white variety, gypsophila Bristol Fairy. This is a lovely sight in June. It reaches three feet or more then but continues into fall to bloom on new growth which never attains more than eighteen inches. Consider this change in height when you plant gypsophila Bristol Fairy.

If you have room for but one variety, let this be it but try to deal in small sizes since gypsophilas form strong, thick tap roots which prefer not to be transplanted. In fact, I always try to obtain potted plants of gypsophila because they move better. Full sun and usually some extra lime in the soil are advisable with removal of faded shoots so new clouds of growth will develop. This cutting of shoots, however, usually occurs before fading since I never have enough babysbreath for bouquets.

The fairly new G. *repens* Rosy Veil is also lovely, flowering two weeks ahead of Bristol Fairy and for just as long but not growing so tall, only to two feet. For the small garden Rosy Veil is good because in every way it is a more limited plant. You can increase your stock of either gypsophila from tip or root cuttings but not from seeds since this hybrid does not come true. A pleasing white for the smaller plot is G. *repens bodgiri*.

Not until late July or early August does my last grace note open in the border. This is the Great Sea Lavender, *Statice latifolia*. It produces from a shining crown of stalwart basal leaves a fine twenty-four-inch lavender cloud which seems never to fade. Even after five weeks or so it will be as fresh and full of color as when it first developed its eighteen-inch perfection.

This lavender, not to be confused with true lavender, *Lavandula* of fragrant memories, always poses a problem. Shall I cut it for a bouquet where in water it will stay fresh for some two weeks or leave it for longer loveliness in the garden? Usually the garden wins out, since what happens outdoors in summer is always more important to me than any bouquet effects inside. (Both statice and the gypsophila variety *paniculata* can also be dried for winter bouquets though I am not very intrigued by such uses.)

This statice, given sun and a sandy soil, seems to be completely happy. It never needs extra water or spraying or anything else beyond average, routine care and it looks so pretty next my yellow snapdragons. A nice child, well behaved and unexacting, I think, as I note its contented condition in the border.

CHAPTER XIII

QUALITY EDGINGS MAKE THE BORDER

"A GARDEN is only as fine as its edges" is one of those pleasant, homely adages which the experienced gardener likes to trot out for the benefit of the novice. Actually no piece of gardening advice I can give is sounder than this which urges the careful selection of first-rate edging plants. For it is certainly true that the general good looks of a planting depend tremendously on the way the beds and borders are terminated. Indeed, during out-of-bloom periods a well-chosen edging will do as much for your garden as a new satin binding on a shabby blanket or a piece of fresh, even fringe sewn along the ends of a worn carpet.

Too often edging plants are after-thoughts whereas they should be important primary considerations. In fact, when I am making a new garden with definite budgeting in mind, I always allocate at the outset what might seem a disproportionate amount to the purchase of high quality edging plants and save by filling in behind them with annuals. This produces a finished appearance even during the first season.

And the possibilities for the purpose are practically endless even though many of the so-called edging plants are not included on my own preferred list. For I feel strongly on the subject of omissions and do not consider worthy any plants which are not, first, either evergreen or of good foliage tendency from spring through fall and, second, of attractive and fairly prolonged blooming habit. In the back of my mind there is always a third criterion which I think of as style.

For the formal garden, distinguished by straight lines or by definite curves and circles and by a certain balanced plan of planting, the evergreen edging plant of permanently neat and distinguished appearance is ideal. Think of varieties for this purpose as "binding" rather than "fringe" plants. They should appear as smooth and straight along the fronts of the beds as lengths of strong green ribbon firmly stretched there.

First choice obviously falls on the slow-growing English boxwood, *Buxus sempervirens suffruticosa*. This box forms the great object lesson of the Williamsburg gardens which during certain off-season periods have little to commend them but their important edges. These alone make them lovely. Despite its beauty this box, however, has certain drawbacks. If where you live, for example, an unsightly burlap screen in winter is going to be essential to its life, omit box by all means. It is expensive too. Where temperatures are not too low, however, and this is the wanted plant, you can develop young specimens from cuttings which if first dipped in one of the root forming hormone substances will in six weeks develop a root system the size of an egg. Then the young plants are set out, and tended for a year in what is termed a "nursery row," that is, a place in the cutting or vegetable garden where care can be easy and constant.

However, because of its capriciousness many of you will not care to be bothered with boxwood. For you there are various beautiful substitutes, some but recently developed and charming enough to rival the older favorite. *Pachistima canbyi*, for example, is a choice dwarf evergreen shrub which does not grow above eight inches tall or eighteen wide. It may be trimmed as a binding plant or left natural as a graceful, feathery fringe. Tolerant of twenty degrees below zero with no tendency to burn or discolor and of equal beauty in sun or light shade, it is first rate wherever an evergreen edging is desired.

Another possibility, if not too tall for the bed to be edged, is the blue-leafed willow, *Salix purpurea nana*, hailing from the Arctic Circle. It can bear those wet or heavy soils which spell demise to most plants and may likewise be enjoyed in a formal or natural state. It is quite possible by judicious pruning to keep the height to twelve inches and the width to eight.

The old-fashioned germander, *Teucrium chamaedrys*, a picturesque, aromatic plant reminiscent of knot-garden days, grows twelve to fifteen inches high. Its glossy green foliage is often mistaken for that of boxwood but the plant is far hardier. This is a delightful substitute.

Then there is English ivy, *Hedera helix*, a gem of a

plant for locations out of full sun. Where the perennial border of the shrubbery line is somewhat shaded, this shining-leaved vine makes a charming binding. It must, of course, be sternly trimmed to check its gadding proclivities. And English ivy has, of course, the great advantage of being very easily and quickly developed from cuttings. The Baltic type has smaller leaves and withstands lower temperatures and a greater degree of sunshine. Thus English boxwood, *pachistima,* the Arctic willow, germander, and English ivies in their natural or sheared state, comprise a most distinguished selection of evergreen edging material for formal plantings.

For the informal border or the garden laid out in balanced beds informally planted, a number of good-foliaged, flowering subjects immediately suggest themselves. Foremost among these is the hardy evergreen candytuft, *Iberis sempervirens.* It has for years, during which I have tried out many other kinds of plants, remained my favorite and this despite the fact that Philadelphia's July weather sometimes brings on attacks of red spider if the plants are not dusted once or twice that month with sulphur or rotenone. I cling to the old-fashioned type, *Iberis sempervirens.* Something of a sprawler, it produces a most soft and lovely fringe for my four oblong flower beds which are in full view at all times from porch and study.

During the growing season this sturdy sub-shrub has no shabby moments, while its six weeks of snowy spring bloom appears, with the yellow and cream narcissi, as the first sweet enchantment of the gardening year. Directly the flowers fade, I sternly shear the plants to keep in line the fresh new growth as it develops. Little Gem and Snowflake are more compact *iberis* varieties while Snowflake bears larger individual blooms. I like either of these compact growers for rather narrow borders.

A number of other flowering plants measure up to my standard of fine foliage and prolonged bloom. Unless the border is over fifty feet long, however, I feel that a stronger effect is achieved by planting but one kind of plant or blending colors of one kind. For example, a border edged entirely with such a Dianthus species as *caesius*, the Cheddar Pink, with its sweet-smelling, rosy May flowers is a delight. Also attractive and so easy to get abundantly from seed is a mixed edging of the old-fashioned clove pink, *Dianthus plumarius.*

For lengthier borders I prefer a rhythm of the plumarius garden pinks in a repeated series of such varieties as the rose-pink Bristol Maid, the crimson-flecked Bristol Jewel, the pale pink Essex Witch, the pure white Her Majesty and the bright rose, crimson-eyed Gladys Cranfield. The series looks best if composed of uneven numbers, that is, three or five different varieties, of five or more plants of each variety to a stretch, and the series repeated at least three times. Only for an over fifty-foot bed, however, is this likely to look well. And with such long lines to fill in, the gardener who is fond of variety may quite rightly select a repeated series of different kinds of plants, such as the double white rockcress, *Arabis alpina floreplenо*, the pale yellow alyssum, *Alyssum saxatile citrinum*, not *compactum*, and the lilac rainbow rockcress, *Aubrietia* eyri.

My own preference except for very extensive plantings is for a one-color, one-variety line-up. For those who, like me, find such a planting restful and not mechanical I suggest, next in quality to the hardy candytuft, the almost evergreen coralbell, Heuchera. Its shapely geranium leaves and slender clouds of pink or white bloom have long been a delight in my garden where foliage is top quality throughout the season and they show considerable shade tolerance.

For shade, however, nothing is prettier than clear yellow primroses of the true English type, *Primula vulgaris.* One small suburban garden I know is thus completely edged, along evergreen and shrub borders as well as flower beds. Behind the primroses are clumps of narcissi in many cream and white varieties. When other gardens are just waking up in April, this one appears in full glory. And through division a few English primrose plants soon go a long way. I like, too, to strengthen the picture with the lavender-blue Jacob's ladder, *Polemonium reptans,* placed in bold clusters among the narcissi. This polemonium, in fact, almost qualifies for edging but its foliage in summer is not quite good enough.

Certain other low-growing plants often suggested for edging I cannot for various reasons recommend. These include the Persian stonecress and Geneva bugle, the forget-me-not anchusa, *Anchusa myosotidiflora,* the fringed bleedingheart, *Dicentra eximia, Phlox divaricata, Iris cristata,* which does not line up well, and the violas, except perhaps Jersey Gem. If future viola varieties prove sufficiently heat-resistant, however, I am all for placing these long-flowering plants on the preferred list.

And don't overlook strawberries. These make an edging which is unusual, dependable and enchanting. Those tiny kinds of the fraise du bois type, we used to eat in France, with heaps of thick, almost sour cream are finds of the first order. One summer I saw a whole garden edged with them, variety Baron Solemacher, and the owner reported constant flowers and fruits from May on to frost.

In selecting anything so important as edging plants, however, it is not wise to depend entirely on anyone's advice. Decide for yourself whether you prefer a "binding" or a "fringe" and consider which seems most suitable for your own garden planting. Then, whether you plan to proceed via seed, cutting, or plant, try to see for yourself just what your preferred plants look like in the nurseryman's row. After all there's no better criterion for such an important selection than your very own eyesight.

❧ ❧

CHAPTER XIV

BIENNIALLY YOURS

BIENNIALS are the puzzlers in our gardens. Sometimes they seem to behave more like annuals because many of them produce an early, if sparse, fall crop of flowers from prompt spring sowings. Often they tend to be perennial, living on from year to year or else appearing to, because they propagate themselves by self-sowing. Indeed, when we want a lot of hollyhocks, foxgloves, Chinese pinks or canterbury bells, the definition of a biennial as a plant which "sown one year, flowers and dies the next" is only moderately helpful. It's individual behavior we must know about and with these particular plants, this varies with the location of our gardens.

My plan, therefore, for a long time has been to treat as biennial those plants which *give the best results* when they are sown one year and harvested the next. The point is that I like everything on my small place to be "in the pink." I have no time to coddle the weary or make strong the faint. So when in my garden the foxglove, so important for early June height, rings out its last sweet steepled bell or the pansy edgings get that exhausted look, I whisk them out with complete finality and fill the precious space again with autumn chrysanthemums or midget marigolds. Meanwhile the double white hollyhocks for me carry on as perennials, producing their charming crêpe paper rosettes year after year in the original lovely form. So they remain undisturbed.

Generally speaking, biennials are more trouble than either annuals or perennials. They take two years of handling to produce what annuals do the same season and their flowering period is then only about as long as that of the average perennial. These are their disadvantages.

In their favor we must admit that biennials include unusually lovely plants which seem to flower just when we need them most. Foxgloves, for example, bring early height in June while the delphiniums are only making up their minds. Sweet william is colorful when the rest of the garden is recovering from its first spring spurt and has not yet gathered strength for summer. Nothing surpasses the canterbury bells for June drama, while the alpine forget-me-not produces a blue cloud which the perennial type never equals.

Where winters are not particularly severe, biennial culture can be simplified to summer sowing in an open seed bed, early autumn transplanting to a reserve bed, and spring setting-out in the border. Where winter temperatures drop to twenty degrees Fahrenheit or lower, a cold frame is required to insure safe dealings with biennials.

I like to concentrate on one or at most two varieties of biennials each year. Then I grow a thumping big crop of the chosen kind. This results in a strong seasonal effect in the garden and reduces sowing and transplanting to a two-day scheme—the days separated by a number of weeks, of course.

I make my plantings as late in the season as the type of biennial allows. This permits sowing when the spring rush of work is past and also reduces care by a couple of months. When possible, I sow after a rain on a cool summer day rather than during a stretch of torrid summer heat which is not conducive to good germination.

Once the seedlings attain their second crop of leaves, which are noticeably different from the first, they are set out at about three-inch intervals in rows in the vegetable garden or else replanted in the cold frame where they were first sown. The soil is now enriched for them with a little balanced plant food and made somewhat heavier too by the addition of more garden loam. This transplanting which occurs before mid-September has a strengthening effect on root systems. In winter if the plants are not to be in a cold frame, they are protected with a covering of crisp oak leaves which do not mat or with an inch or so of finely pulverized peat moss. Varieties with green tops have the covering pulled around them and *under* their crowns, not above them. If left in the cold frame they are lightly covered in November but the glass is not fastened down until after the first hard freeze. After the New Year it is raised during warm sunnv afternoons for fifteen minutes or so at a stretch.

These are the biennials which I have found worth while: Chinese pinks, canterbury bells, forget-me-nots, foxgloves, hollyhocks, honesty, Iceland poppies, Siberian wallflowers, sweet williams and violas. For English daisies and pansies raised at home I have only a maybe-so feeling.

The Chinese pinks, *Dianthus chinensis* or *heddewigi*, may be sown the third week in June. Then they flower lightly by September with a much stronger display prepared for next summer. Once they are established in your garden you can count on them to flower from early spring until late fall. They are fine for bouquets, spicily fragrant and excellent for bedding. Best sown where they are to grow, they are thinned out in April. Indispensable for the cutting garden, they are not to be confused with such truly perennial pinks as *Dianthus plumarius*.

Probably the handsomest of all biennials are the canterbury bells, both the single *Campanula medium* and *C. calycantha*, the double or cup-and-saucer variety. Both come in particularly good purple shades, also in rose and white. My vote goes to the calycanthas in "dark blue" and lots of them. These are biennials to be sown before the end of July, moved before crowding to a reserve bed or slatted cold frame with afternoon shade and finally transplanted the next spring after growth has started but before buds are set, to the borders. Almost three feet high, they flower in late May and June. Some supplementary summer bloom is later produced from basal shoots but I am not inclined to keep the campanulas after the height of their effect is past, preferring to use their space for summer-flowering nicotiana or miniature dahlias. If the handsome chimney bellflower, *Campanula pyramidalis*, does not stay by you, it too must be given this biennial treatment.

Forget-me-nots are one of the choicest of the smaller flowering biennials. The variety *Myosotis dissitiflora* is a sky blue gem to be introduced into the garden at your earliest possible convenience. Let it go to seed there each year and from April into June you will have something special in the way of a true blue foil for tulip and daffodil. Plan for late July or early August sowing. It will be worth while to prevent any tendency to damping off by sterilizing the seed bed first. These forget-me-nots, sown in place, readily winter in the open even where it is very cold. You will bless the day you established this delicate blue charmer in your garden.

The most important biennials are probably the foxgloves because they give height to the garden composition early in the season. The giant Shirley Hybrids of digitalis produce in June stately four- to six-foot steeples of crimson-spotted white to rose blooms. There are also pure white and rose varieties as well as Sutton's Apricot and Primrose, both charming with blue flax and such a late yellow narcissus as Cleopatra. The fine seed is sown thinly before the end of July and the young plants set out six weeks later, ten inches apart, in row or frame. Foxgloves require a lot of water through the summer to avoid any possible check to growth. They are wintered in the same manner as canterbury bells and moved in spring with a good ball of earth.

The althaeas or hollyhocks are almost too rampant for the border since they require nearly three feet for each plant but they are perfect in a generous corner by themselves, or in bold groups associated with shrubs. Single mixed kinds are no trouble whatever. They grow five to seven feet high, flower from mid-July to mid-August and, if there is good drainage, either survive or resow very freely. If you want choice doubles, see first if the roots prove winter hardy for you. If not, then treat them strictly as biennials. I found that one color, preferably salmon pink or white, of the doubles at a time was an effective plan. If several colors are grown and self-sowing permitted, the bees arrange an interesting cross-fertilization program for you. Hollyhocks, one of the most robust of the biennials, need not be sown until early August.

The shining silver seed pods of honesty or *Lunaria* are far more important than the violet and white spring flowers. So consider this biennial for cutting in the fall when you can do lovely arrangement things with it in pewter. Not an important biennial, it is a nice extra for sowing in August.

Seldom listed as biennial, the Iceland poppy, *Papaver nudicaule*, gives best results for me when so treated. It is a small darling bearing crinkle-petaled cups on twelve-inch stems all through spring and early summer and sporadically thereafter if seed pods are removed. These poppies look well in the border behind the hardy candytuft and between the narcissus colonies.

The bright orange of the Siberian wallflower, *Cheiranthus allioni*, has a sparkling April effect on a spring border which features Leedsi narcissus and the subtle blues of Virginia bluebells, violets, and *Phlox divaricata*. The plants grow twelve to eighteen inches tall and because of a fibrous root system are able to withstand transplanting easily. I like to sow them early in July and transplant in September to a reserve garden row. Then in early spring I move them to the border after the bulbs and perennials are in evidence there. September placement is not very practical because what looks like a vacancy then may be actually a dormant mertensia plant. The Siberian wall-flower winters healthily in the open.

The old-fashioned spotty sweet william, *Dianthus barbatus*, is easy enough to keep in abundance either because the roots remain or there is self-seeding. And these have pleasing flowers too for a cutting row. For borders, where color schemes matter a lot to me, I prefer separate sowings of Newport Pink, Sutton's Pink Beauty, Giant Pure White or Scarlet Beauty. Sometimes plants of these too last more than one season, more often they "revert" or rather a seedling crop develops from a faded flower I didn't cut in time. As far as behavior goes, it seems that the best sweet william turns out to be biennial rather than perennial. And it is one of the very easiest. A grand crop can be readily obtained from a late June sowing in an open seed bed in almost any location.

Happy the gardeners who can depend on *Viola cornuta* for perennial effect but we are all too few. This is a crop which flowers freely the second year from April sowing but heat prostration is likely to get the plant down the next summer. Violas, except perhaps a very few like Jersey Gem, therefore prove more satisfactory when grown biennially for April, May and June effect. If you live where summers are very hot, permit them to make a quick and dignified exit and don't waste time on summer mulching, clipping, feeding and soaking. Results are not worth the effort. For spring and early summer, however, violas are delightful for edging, while small petunias, perhaps, are being perfected elsewhere. Awkwright Ruby, Apricot, and Blue Perfection are viola varieties which have given me much pleasure.

As for English daisies, *Bellis perennis*, to be sown in early August, they do make a charming edge if enough plants of a variety like Snowball can be raised to outline the whole garden. Cold frame quarters and careful attention to ventilation in early spring are, however, essential to bring them into full flower early enough in April for them to perform well before hot weather. For me this is a much too arduous crop to attempt when anything as attractive and final as hardy candytuft is mine for the one raising.

I feel the same about pansies of which I prefer to buy some flowering plants each spring. They are not worth growing tediously from seed unless there are enough cold frames in which to winter them. This is not because they are not cold-weather tolerant—actually it's our roaring summers which prevent their permanence, not the winter's cold. But to get the most out of pansies, they must be forced to finest flower by early April. Grown in the open, this does not seem possible. If you go in for them, sow them in August. Big blooms are dependent on variety rather than on special culture, so consider Coronation Gold, Lake of Thun or Snow White. Even one frame of these provides distinguished spring accompaniment. Mixtures and small-flowering kinds have charm—all pansies do—but they are not very telling for an important edging position though always nice to cut.

Here then are a dozen possible biennials for you to consider. Do pick at least one for planting this summer and the next time something you like is marked Biennial in the catalogue, don't be mystified. It's really either a long-lived annual or short-term perennial and you now know how to manage either.

CHAPTER XV

GROWN TO BE GATHERED

THE cutting section is by rights an extremely personal, if not a prejudiced aspect of the garden. It is not meant for display. Therefore eye-searing mixtures and one-of-each plantings are conveniently in order there. It is meant, however, to supply its individual owner with just what she desires all through the year for her house arrangements, as well as for her bouquets. I must include these since simple bunches of flowers are also a highly respectable part of interior decorating and a most comforting inclusion for those who still feel uncertain about their technique of arrangement. When, however, arrangements are taken seriously by those who frankly state, "I only plant to pick," then generous space is allotted for cutting and other perennial plantings are omitted.

In your plot, plant only according to your needs. Have in mind the color schemes of the rooms your bouquets will adorn and the months when an abundance will not be wasted. If, for instance, you spend August in the mountains, let the lull come there.

Choose some flowers just for fragrance. A jardiniere of

the pale pink peony Marie Crousse, for instance, will be a delight if placed on a deep window sill at the landing where it will perfume the halls, upstairs and down. And keep in mind variety of form. Since globular flowers predominate, plant for contrast, spikes of aconite, lupine, thermopsis and delphinium, though the last is a "faller." And have clouds of babysbreath, sea lavender, coralbell and the gray-leaved artemisia Silver King, for blending. If you in your house have space for great telling massive bouquets, freely grow the coarse sunflowers and asters but if your rooms are small select for cutting in-scale material, the delicately-wrought bleedinghearts, the refined oriental iris and the graceful anemones.

My cutting garden when most satisfactory to me has certainly been a conglomeration. I have, for instance, three plants of single crimson hollyhocks for the great blue stone jar I place on the piano in hot weather when the summer living room needs warm accents to relieve its cool muted grays and greens. There is a half row of geum Red Wings, and two plants of helenium Chippersfield Orange for the same purpose. I have a whole row of assorted "fillers" and gray-leaved material and a half row of the rampant feverfew, *Matricaria*. I wouldn't think of letting this loose in my tidy borders but I prize it highly for white urn arrangements in early July. Then it is companion to yellow daylily and blue hydrangea. With a passion for white I have a whole sparkling area reserved for shastas in four varieties, a generous space for delphinium Galahad and, in the shade, a great satisfying spread of the white August lily, *Hosta*. This arranged in a clear green glass bowl surrounded by a frill of its own waxen heart-shaped leaves appears as cool as a lily pond in the yellow dining room. Finally I have at least fifty chrysanthemum plants, more than any well-balanced gardener would select for such a modest place, but chrysanthemums happen to be my hobby, so the cutting garden, being mine, is plotted to my individual taste.

In laying out yours, consider the most favorable location none too good, since you are expecting a heavy year-round perennial crop from this one plot. Select a southeastern location if possible, with a spot of light shade for the spring crop. Don't be afraid of size since a garden laid out in rows easily permits every necessary process of gardening—cultivating, watering, feeding and spraying—to be an easy, straightforward, up-one-row-and-down-the-next business.

For the sake of the over-all view, however, place some neat regular boundaries. A picket fence is pleasing if it suits the architecture of your house, or the plot may be outlined with shrubs or evergreens which also yield material for cutting. If the area is quite small, however, it will be unwise to surround it with tall strong material which tends to cut off air and light. I like my peony boundary on one side because it is attractive all season and gives me the kind of lavish display of peonies I want for a house with deep window sills where large bouquets are always in order. Boxwood then on the other three sides looks well because it fits the cutting oblong into the general scheme of our place. Otherwise it might appear that I had dropped this great block of color down on one corner of the lawn just for the fun of it. A cutting garden despite its highly useful and specialized character needs thus to be related by proper boundaries to whatever else exists on the property.

If you have shade, plant there material for spring cutting. Plan for many small at-the-elbow bouquets of basket-of-gold, rockcress, English primrose and candytuft, and for the table, grow bleedinghearts, columbines and doronicum to go with your tulips. A clump of Apricot hemerocallis in May and a row of white Gudrun, blue Sensation and yellow Alta California iris, plus some Siberian iris, will, when set in the sun, richly supply the hall. And, of course, at this time there can never be too many lilies-of-the-valley and sweet violets. These indispensables, however, can usually be placed elsewhere on a property. They are not row by row growers.

For late spring and early summer, select peonies, one of each color you like in early, midseason and late varieties. Six plants will yield richly. Be sure to pick the pale ones in bud so they will hold their delicate coloring indoors. Think, too, for this season of fragrant astilbe, sweet rocket, garden heliotrope, pinks and carnations. Veronica, gas plant, Chinese delphinium, and baptisia are fine spikes and, of course, there must be oriental iris. Nepeta is feathery and soft for variety while many of the daisies like the shastas, coreopsis, pyrethrum and Sherbrook gaillardias, starting now, conveniently continue to frost.

These in midsummer are supplemented by scabiosa, stokesia, helenium, coneflower and sunflower. Physostegia and hollyhocks are good spires while the various hostas prove unexpectedly handsome. Phlox you can have if you will, but like delphinium it requires constant cleaning up.

For autumn, hardy ageratum is a good filler. So are hardy asters with aconites for accents. For final grandeur, there are anemones and chrysanthemums in as many forms and colors as your space permits. Nor are they really final, if you have Christmas and Lenten roses in a sheltered place outdoors to carry you through to spring or *Iris stylosa* in one cold frame for December and January and sweet violets in another for March.

The most lasting bouquets you will discover are composed of hellebores—three weeks one January for mine—chrysanthemum, hardy aster, columbine, scabiosa, shasta daisy, pyrethrum, stokesia and doronicum. All bouquets, however, last longer if you avoid drafty places and a hot, dry atmosphere. Shallow bowls, provided they are kept filled, are as good as deep ones since there is only one point of water intake—the stem. Cut this on a long slant to increase the area of absorption.

Then, before arranging, steep your cut flowers in cold water for at least an hour, or overnight if you can. Place them in a deep vessel set in a cool spot. Forty-five to fifty degrees is fine in winter and spring, while the shady porch is a good hot weather approximation. Wilted flowers often revive completely after this steeping. Be sure to remove all foliage below the water line of your arrangements and to prolong life clip the stems and change the water daily. The shorter the stem, it appears, the longer the keeping.

Unless flowers are scarce, however, this is a chore you needn't feel you must face. Plenty of bouquets stay attractive the better part of a week if some fresh water is added daily. On the principle of arresting the maturing life cycle of flowers and so retarding their wilting, Professor Alex Laurie of Ohio State University, who has investigated this whole matter, also recommends the addition of certain chemicals to the water. Commercially these are procurable as Bloomlife and Floralife. Follow directions with these and you will be surprised at the longevity your lovely arrangements will achieve.

❧ ❧

CHAPTER XVI

FLOWERS FOR CHURCH YARD AND ALTAR

THE planting of the church property and the adornment of the altar are the natural concern of all the gardening members of a congregation. Yet how often this pleasant obligation is completely overlooked by those whose own homes are never without colorful flower arrangements! In fact, I recently attended a church in a community where many of the members had unusually handsome gardens but where the entrance to their place of worship was bordered by an indifferent barberry hedge and surrounded by a most meager grass plot. In the bright month of September there was not a flower to be seen. Furthermore, whoever had filled the altar vases that Sunday had little knowledge of the keeping qualities of various materials since through the entire sermon from autumn branches of japonica one piece of fruit after another dropped in loud and awful succession.

In a number of communities, however, there seems to be an awakening of the value of gardens in church yards whether these be open to public view or in enclosures.

Certainly members who give time to the planting and maintenance of such gardens discover they have a rich and continuous reward in the appreciation of the entire congregation. For we all experience a gracious uplifting of spirit and a quieting of mind, a kind of preparation for service, when our path to the church door lies between lines of fragrant peonies or glowing drifts of chrysanthemums. Indeed, what visitor to Stoke Poges will ever forget the sweetly burdened rose trees which form a step-by-step accompaniment to the door of that ancient little

THE CHURCH YARD WELCOMES GARDENING HANDS.

English church made famous by Gray's Elegy? It is also pleasant at any time, weekday or Sunday, to leave a busy street for a brief time of meditation in a secluded church yard garden serene with the beauty of larkspur and lily.

If the making of such a garden is a new undertaking in your community, you will find it a good plan in the beginning to use perennials which are to a degree lasting and undemanding. A peony path with plantings of narcissus between the plants would be a long delight in spring and require little but routine care thereafter. If the property is small, however, this would be too space-consuming a selection. A broad border edged with hardy candytuft and filled with intermediate and taller iris and summer phlox would give a better through-the-season effect.

In one small cloistered garden I know, where a seasonal choice had to be made, spring is passed over but from June on color is constant and the deep corner plantings are bright masses of bloom. Pink hollyhocks, belladonna delphinium, regal and candidum lilies, oriental and Shirley poppies and various yellow daylilies with self-sowing September Jewel chrysanthemums weave a brilliant tapestry. Paths are edged with dwarf marigolds, portulaca and ageratum. An interested Committee for the Garden maintains this lovely plot which was started with plants from the members' own gardens. None of this material is cut since its outdoor value is so deeply enjoyed.

When the church property is large enough to support a cutting as well as a landscape garden, that is an ideal situation. One flower committee not finding this possible, however, worked out an uncomplicated but most satisfactory plan for supplying the altar without drawing upon its cloister plantings. A list was made of the most useful flowers for church decoration. These were apportioned to the committee members for separate growing. Then without telephoning or further consultation the person responsible for a given Sunday was privileged to go where, according to her list, the current supply was to be found and to pick what she required.

Experience soon indicates what flowers are effective and which colors most telling. Blues and violets which first come to mind as fitting, must frequently be omitted since these gray out completely in the dimness of a church interior. But red, pink, yellow and quantities of white are invaluable with plenty of large greens for background. Particularly if vases stand against a figured wall must there be a screen of rhododendrons or something similar in the back of the vase to set off the flowers. An unusually beautiful arrangement is possible with magnolia branches placed to silhouette madonna or regal lilies. The green leaves are oiled a little to give them gleaming highlights.

In arranging church flowers it is wise to strive for broad masses and to avoid spotting, which is unpleasantly obvious the farther back one sits. Since so many view the flowers a long way off, the final effect must be tested from the very rear of the church. Suitable and beautiful arrangements are possible with these perennials: peonies, August lilies, chrysanthemums, oriental poppies, iris, anemones, hardy asters, and most of the coarser daisies. Delicate things like columbines do not carry enough weight.

Delphinium and phlox are also better left out because they are poor keepers. Since the vases must usually be filled and placed on Saturday and left in a close atmosphere until morning, it is important to select flowers which last well. These may then be carefully prepared (see page 190) so that they will hold up as long as possible, both in the church and later when they are taken to the sick. On Sunday morning it is a good precaution to add some fresh water. It would be better, of course, to change it completely but that usually involves disturbance of the carefully wrought arrangement.

Memorial gifts to most churches fill the vases, of course, on many Sundays. Even so, many supplementary flowers are needed and it seems a pity that these should always be bought or even that memorials should not sometimes be grown rather than purchased. The gift that is grown is somehow more lovingly offered while that church is certainly richer which is regularly adorned through the efforts of its own gardening members.

LISTS FOR READY REFERENCE

I

Cultural Index to Valuable Perennials

Name Botanical and Common	Height in Feet	Color	Season of Bloom	Remarks
Achillea				
eupatorium	3	Yellow	July–September	Coarse, dry places, for border and cutting
ptarmica, Snowball	2	White	July–September	
Aconitum				
fisheri	2–3	Purple	September and October	Shade, not drought resistant, lovely when they thrive
sparksi	4–5	Dark blue	July and August	
wilsoni	6–7	Deepest	October and November	
Adam's Needle (*Yucca*)				
Althaea rosea	5–7	All but blue	July and August	Requires much space
Alyssum saxatile citrinum	1	Pale yellow	April and May	Fine edging plants
Anchusa				
Dropmore	4–5	Blue	June	Valuable tall blue
myosotidiflora	1	Blue	May and June	Brilliant, dwarf, invaluable
Anemone japonica	2–3	Red, pink, white	September and November	Among best for autumn

Name Botanical and Common	Height in Feet	Color	Season of Bloom	Remarks
Aquilegia				
caerulea	1½	Lavender	April–July	Dainty, airy plants for border contrast and cutting
chrysantha	2½	Yellow	May–July	
Crimson Star	2	Red and white	May–August	
Flabellata nana alba	2–3	White	May and June	
Scott Elliott hybrids	1½–2	Mixed	May–July	
Arabis alpina florepleno	½	White	April	Edging, early
Artemisia Silver King	3	Gray foliage		Good gray mist for "peace-making"
Asperula odorata	1	White	May	Fragrant, shade
Aster, Hardy		All but yellow	September–October	Essential, autumn border background, lacy effect in bloom
Novae-angliae	2½–5			
Novi-belgi	2–4			
Astilbe	1½–4	White to red	June–August	Shade, marvelous plant
August Lily (*Hosta*)				
Babysbreath (*Gypsophila*)				
Bachelor's Button (*Centaurea*)				
Balloonflower (*Platycodon*)				
Baptisia	2	Blue	June	Foliage and flower good
Betonica	2–3	Purple	June, July, August	For dry places, coarse

Blanket Flower (*Gaillardia*)				
Bleedingheart (*Dicentra*)				
Bocconia	5–6	White	June–September	Coarse, use with shrubs
Boltonia	5–6	White	August–September	Like wild aster. Divide every spring
Campanula				
calycantha	2½	Pink, white, purple	June	Biennial cup and saucer type
carpatica	1	Blue, white	June–October	Edging, snip faded flowers
medium	2½	Purple, pink, white	June	Large bells on stalks, biennial
persicifolia	2½	Purple, white	June–July	Peach bell type
pyramidalis	4–6	Purple, white	June–September	Important delphinium supplement
Canterbury Bell (*Campanula medium*)				
Carnation (*Dianthus caryophyllus*)				
Centaurea				
macrocephala	3½	Yellow	July–August	Thistle-like blooms
montana	2	Blue	May–September	Sturdy
Cheiranthus allioni	1–1½	Orange	April	Easily moved among bulbs
Chrysanthemum	1–3	All but blue	September–December	Fall indispensables (See chart, p. 146)
maximum	1½	White	June–November	Fine white cut flower

Name Botanical and Common	Height in Feet	Color	Season of Bloom	Remarks
Cimicifuga racemosa	4–6	White	July–August	Shade and moisture
Columbine (*Aquilegia*)				
Convallaria majalis	1	White	May	Fragrance, shade
Coralbells (*Heuchera*)				
Coreopsis	2½	Yellow	June–September	Undistinguished, reliable
Cornflower (*Centaurea*)				
Cup and Saucer (*Campanula calycantha*)				
Daylily (*Hemerocallis or Hosta*)				
Delphinium				
chinense	2½–3	Blue, white	June–October	Good blue, constant bloom
hybrids	3–6	Blue, pink, lavender, white	June–November	Exceptional blue, temperamental
Dianthus		Red, pink, white		Lime and grit in soil
barbatus	1		June	Usually biennial
caesius	½–1	Rose only	May	Fragrant cheddar pink
caryophyllus	1		June–September	More humus in soil, fragrant
chinensis			May–October	Usually biennial
latifolius	1–1½		June–September	Cluster form
plumarius	1–1½		May	Fragrant grass pink, old-fashioned type

Dicentra		Rose		
eximia	1		May–October	Plumy type, sun or shade, persistent foliage
spectabilis	2		April–June	Handsome, but summer disappearance, shade
Dictamnus	2½	Pink, white	June–July	Permanent placement
Digitalis				
ambigua	2–3	Yellow	June–July	Wild garden, perennial
gloxinaeflora	4–6	White, rose		Usually biennial
Isabellina	3–4	Pale yellow		Perennial, fine
Doronicum	1–1½	Yellow	April–May	Summer disappearance
Eupatorium	1½	Lavender	August–Frost	Sun or shade, cutting, rampant
Evening Primrose (*Oenothera*)				
Feverfew (*Matricaria*)				
Flax (*Linum*)				
Forget-me-not (*Myosotis*)				
Funkia (*Hosta*)				
Gaillardia	2	Red, yellow	June–November	Drought enduring
Gas Plant (*Dictamnus*)				
Garden Heliotrope (*Valeriana*)				
Gay Feather (*Liatris*)				
Gerbera	1½	Yellow, pink, orange	June–September	Cold frame wintering

Name Botanical and Common	Height in Feet	Color	Season of Bloom	Remarks
Geum	2	Orange, red	May–October	Moisture, brilliant
Globeflower (*Trollius*)				
Gypsophila				
Bristol Fairy	3–4	White	June–October	Essential for garden misting and bouquets
repens, bodgiri	2	White		
repens, Rosy Veil	2	Pink		
Hardy Ageratum (*Eupatorium*)				
Helenium	1½–4	Yellow to red	July–October	Showy, divide every spring
Helen's Flower (*Helenium*)				
Helianthus	4	Yellow	August–October	Coarse plant dahlia flower
Heliopsis	3–5	Yellow, orange	July–November	Strong, fine to cut
Helleborus	1–2	Pink, white	November–April	Moisture, shade
Hemerocallis	1½–4½	Yellow, orange	May–October	See chart p. 127
Hesperis matronalis	3	White, lavender	June–September	Fragrant
Heuchera	1–1½	Rose, white	May–September	Edging, splendid plant
Hibiscus	3–4	Red, pink, white	July–September	Enormous, hollyhock-like
Hollyhock (*Althaea*)				
Hosta	1½–2	White, blue	July–August	Fine foliage, fragrance
Iberis	1	White	April–June	Evergreen edging

Iceland Poppy (*Papaver nudicaule*)				
Iris				See chart p. 80
bearded	2–4½	Various	May–June	Familiar bearded type
cristata	½	Lavender	April	Shade
intermediate	1½	Various	May	Fine forerunner
kaempferi	2½–4	Various	June–July	Handsome flat blooms
Siberian	3–4	Purple, white	May–June	Foliage grassy
Japanese Iris (*Kaempferi*)				
Larkspur (*Delphinium*)				
Leopardbane (*Doronicum*)				
Liatris	4–5	Purple, white	September	Excellent spires
Linum perenne	1½	Blue	May–August	Delicate, airy growth
Lupine (*Lupinus*)				
Lupinus polyphyllus	3	Blue, pink, white	June	Some later blooms
Mallow (*Hibiscus*)				
Matricaria	1½	White	June–October	Tiny daisy, bouquet filler
Meadowrue (*Thalictrum*)				
Mertensia	1–1½	Blue to pink	April	Enchanting for shade
Michaelmas Daisy (*Aster*)				
Mistflower (*Eupatorium*)				
Monarda	2–3	Pink, white, red		Fragrant foliage, rampant
Monkshood (*Aconitum*)				

Name Botanical and Common	Height in Feet	Color	Season of Bloom	Remarks
Myosotis		Blue	April–June	Prefer damp location
alpestris dissitiflora	½			May be biennial
palustris sempeafloresis	½			Perennial type
Nepeta mussini	1–2	Lavender	April–August	Gray foliage, soft effect
Oenothera				
missouriensis	1	Yellow	June–August	Sandy soil, evening flowers
Paeonia				
albiflora	2–3	Red, pink, white, yellow	May–June	Familiar, fine foliage
moutan	3–4	Same colors	May	Tree peony species
officinalis	2–2½	Red	Late May	Old-fashioned "piney"
tenuifolia	1½	Crimson	May	Finely cut leaf
Papaver				
nudicaule	1–1½	Yellow, scarlet, pink, white	May–October	Often biennial
orientale	2–3	Red, pink, white	May–June	See chart p. 100
Peachbell (*Campanula*)				
Penstemon	1½–3	Scarlet, pink white, blue	June–September	Several fine named varieties
Pink (*Dianthus*)				
Plume poppy (*Bocconia*)				
Poppy (*Papaver*)				

Phlox				See chart, p. 109
amoena	⅓	Rose	April, May, September	Evergreen, creeping
arendsi	1½	Lavender	May–June	Shade tolerant
decussata	2–4	All but yellow	June–October	Hardy summer phlox
divaricata	1	Lavender	May	Indispensable for shade
subulata	½	Rose, purple, white	April and May	Creeping mat-like growth
suffruticosa	2–4	All but yellow	June–October	Early tall phlox, fine
Physostegia	1½–4	Pink, rose	July–September	Coarse, reliable for cutting
Platycodon grandiflorum	1½	Purple, white	May–October	Fine for foreground
Plumbago larpentae	1	Deep blue	August–October	Good edger, late growth
Polemonium reptans	½	Blue	May–June	Charming and delicate
Primula vulgaris	¾	Yellow	April–May	Edging for shade
Pyramid bellflower (*Campanula*)				
Pyrethrum roseum	2	Rose, red	May, June	Fine to cut
Rockcress (*Arabis*)				
Rudbeckia			July–September	Never failing
The King	3	Crimson		
White Lustre	3	White		

Name Botanical and Common	Height in Feet	Color	Season of Bloom	Remarks
Salvia				
azurea	3–4	Light blue	August–September	Fine for late true blue
pitcheri	3–4	Deep blue	August–September	More branching
Scabiosa caucasica	1½	Lavender	June–October	Nice to cut
Sea Lavender (*Statice*)				
Shasta Daisy (*Chrysanthemum maximum*)				
Snakeroot (*Cimicifuga*)				
Speedwell (*Veronica*)				
Spiraea (*Astilbe*)				
Statice latifolia	1½	Sea lavender	July–August	Good for misting, green crown
Stokesia	1½	Lavender, white	July–August	Lasting cut flower
Sweet Rocket (*Hesperis*)				
Sweet William (*Dianthus*)				
Sunflower (*Helianthus* or *Heliopsis*)				
Transvaal Daisy (*Gerbera*)				
Thalictrum				
glaucum	5	Yellow	June–July	Spring background
Thermopsis				
caroliniana	5	Yellow	June–July	Lupine-like

Trollius				
Lemon Queen	2	Yellow	May–July	Rich blooming in shade with moisture
Orange Globe	2	Orange	May–July	
Valeriana *officinalis*	4	Blush white	June–July	Heliotrope scent
Veronica				Clean, foreground plant
Blue Spires	2	Purple	June–August	
longifolia subsessilis	2	Purple	July–September	
Viola *cornuta*	½	Yellow, white, purple	April–October	Some varieties not heat resistant
Woodruff (*Asperula*)				
Yarrow (*Achillea eupatorium*)				
Yucca *filamentosa*	6	White	June–July	Large coarse accent

II

Colors by the Dozen

In selecting plants listed below, consider variety descriptions carefully, both in the separate chapters in this book and in the catalogue from which you are ordering.

White

Althaea (Hollyhock)
Anemone japonica (Windflower)
Aster (Michaelmas Daisy)
Chrysanthemum
Chrysanthemum maximum (Shasta Daisy)
Funkia subcordata grandiflora (August Lily)
Gypsophila (Babysbreath)
Iberis sempervirens (Hardy Candytuft)
Iris
Paeonia (Peony)
Papaver orientale (Oriental Poppy)
Phlox

True Blue

Anchusa (Alkanet)
Baptisia (False Indigo)
Centaurea (Cornflower)
Delphinium
Linum (Flax)
Lupinus (Lupine)
Myosotis (Forget-me-not)
Plumbago (Leadwort)
Polemonium (Jacob's Ladder)
Pulmonaria (Lungwort)
Salvia (Meadow Sage)

Lavender and Purple

Aquilegia (Columbine)
Aster (Michaelmas Daisy)
Aster frikarti (Wonder of Staffa)
Campanula (Bellflower)
Delphinium
Eupatorium (Hardy ageratum)
Iris
Mertensia (Virginia Bluebell)
Phlox
Statice latifolia (Sea Lavender)
Stokesia (Cornflower Aster)
Veronica (Speedwell)

Pink

Althaea (Hollyhock)
Aquilegia (Columbine)
Aster (Michaelmas Daisy)
Campanula (Bellflower)
Dianthus (Pinks)
Chrysanthemum
Dictamnus (Gas Plant)
Dicentra (Bleedingheart)
Paeonia (Peony)
Phlox
Papaver orientale (Oriental Poppy)
Lupinus (Lupine)

Yellow

Alyssum
Chrysanthemum
Coreopsis (Tickseed)

Gaillardia (Blanket Flower)
Helenium (Helen's Flower)
Helianthus (Sunflower)
Hemerocallis (Daylily)
Iris
Oenothera (Evening Primrose)
Primula (Primrose)
Thalictrum (Meadowrue)
Thermopsis

Orange and Bronze

Chrysanthemum
Gaillardia (Blanket Flower)
Gerbera (Transvaal Daisy)
Geum
Helenium (Helen's Flower)
Heliopsis (Sunflower)
Hemerocallis (Daylily)
Papaver orientale (Oriental Poppy)
Penstemon (Beard Tongue)
Rudbeckia (Coneflower)
Tritoma (Red Hot Poker)
Trollius (Globeflower)

Cerise and Red

Althaea (Hollyhock)
Aster (Michaelmas Daisy)
Chrysanthemum
Dianthus (Pinks)
Gaillardia (Blanket Flower)
Helenium (Helen's Flower)
Lychnis (Campion)
Monarda (Beebalm)

Paeonia (Peony)
Papaver orientale (Oriental Poppy)
Pyrethrum (Painted Daisy)
Phlox

III

Spreaders for Cutting or Massing

These are to be introduced to the border only after due consideration of their present and future space requirements. Since they are all desirable subjects and especially useful when great masses of cut flowers are wanted, they can often be planted to advantage among shrubs or in odd corners or sections rather than in the herbaceous border where more controlled material looks better and is easier to handle.

Achillea (Yarrow)
Althaea (Hollyhock)
Boltonia asteroides (False Chamomile)
Bocconia cordata (Plume Poppy)
Coreopsis grandiflora (Tickseed)
Eupatorium (Hardy Ageratum)
Helenium (Helen's Flower)
Helianthus (Perennial Sunflower)
Heliopsis (Orange Sunflower)
Hibiscus (Mallow)
Monarda (Beebalm or Bergamot)
Physostegia (False Dragonhead)
Rudbeckia (Coneflower)
Salvia (Meadow Sage)
Valeriana (Garden Heliotrope)

IV

Shade-Tolerant Beauties

Try to consider shade an opportunity rather than a problem and you will discover that you can create many a charming effect not at all possible in the blaze of the sun. Under an apple tree, for example, set bleedinghearts, Virginia bluebells, spireas and forget-me-nots with colonies of narcissis among them. Such a planting is one of the most delightful spots in my spring garden.

All the perennials listed below will bloom in the light open shade of fruit trees, hickory, red birch and dogwood. If you are planning a balanced garden layout, part in sun and part in shade, select plants only from the shade-endured list. These like the sun too and will thrive both ways for you.

If the whole garden is shaded, select from both shade-enduring and shade-preference lists, placing plants from the second group where shadow is strong. In areas of little light, depend upon green alone. The lady ferns and many of their kin will there delight you. Be mindful, however, of soil conditions. Especially if the shaded area is dry, must you do considerable conditioning with humus.

Shade-Endured

Anchusa
Anemone (Windflower)
Aquilegia (Columbine)
Aster (Michaelmas Daisy)
Campanula (Bellflower)
Chrysanthemum
Dictamnus (Gas Plant)
Digitalis (Foxglove)
Doronicum (Leopardbane)

Eupatorium (Hardy Ageratum)
Hemerocallis (Daylily)
Heuchera (Coralbells)
Hibiscus (Mallow)
Iberis (Hardy Candytuft)
Iris
Monarda (Beebalm)
Nepeta (Catmint)
Oenothera (Evening Primrose)
Paeonia (Peony)
Phlox
Physostegia (False Dragonhead)
Platycodon (Chinese Bellflower)
Polemonium (Jacob's Ladder)
Thalictrum (Meadowrue)
Trollius (Globeflower)
Veronica (Speedwell)
Viola

Shade-Preferred

Aconitum (Monkshood)
Asperula (Woodruff)
Astilbe (Spiraea)
Cimicifuga (Snakeroot)
Convallaria (Lily-of-the-valley)
Dicentra (Bleedingheart)
Hosta (*Funkia* or August Lily)
Iris cristata
Mertensia (Virginia Bluebell)
Myosotis (Forget-me-not)
Primula (Primrose)
Trillium
Viola (Violet)

V

Flowers for Fragrance

Fragrance is a blessing added to beauty in many perennial species and in some varieties. When the fine qualities of two varieties are equal, if one is scented, by all means select that one. A garden is lovelier too if some plants are included just for the aromatic quality of their foliage. Especially in the night garden is fragrance desirable and for all plantings which are near the porch or beside frequently open doors or windows of the house. A breeze bearing the sweetness of garden heliotrope or the spiciness of pinks is delightful in the dining room while a bouquet of lilies-of-the-valley or of lemon lilies in the hall is pleasant to come home to. Near the porch let the white August *hostas, Festiva maxima* peonies or Lingard phlox perfume each hour of contemplation and rest. Gardens where only fragrant flowers are welcome have proved a deep delight.

Aquilegia chrysantha (Columbine)
  caerulea
Artemisia
  abrotanum (Southernwood) aromatic leaf
  vulgaris lactiflora
Asperula odorata (Sweet Woodruff)
Astilbe (Spiraea)
Centaurea imperialis (Giant Sweet Sultan)
Cheiranthus (Wallflower)
  allioni
  cheiri
Chrysanthemum
  Burgundy
  Hebe
  Lavender Lady
  Mars
  North Star
  Saladin
  Silver Moon
  Vulcan

Convallaria majalis (Lily-of-the-valley)
Dianthus
barbatus (Sweet William)
caryophyllus (Carnations)
caesius (Cheddar Pink)
hybridus (Sweet Wivelsfield)
plumarius (Grass Pinks)
Dictamnus albus (Gas Plant) aromatic leaf
Hemerocallis (Daylily)
aurantiaca
citrina
dumortieri
flava
Hemerocallis varieties

Apricot	Hyperion	Patricia
Dauntless	Mikado	

Hesperis matronalis (Sweet Rocket)
Hosta subcordata grandiflora (White Daylily or Corfu Lily)
Iris
Eros
Missouri
Pallida dalmatica, Princess Beatrice
Shining Waters
Lavandula vera (True Lavender) aromatic leaf
Monarda didyma (Beebalm) aromatic leaf
Nepeta mussini (Catmint) aromatic leaf
Oenothera missouriensis (Evening Primrose)
Paeonia (Peony)

Alice Harding	La France
Baroness Shroeder	Le Cygne
Couronne d'Or	Mrs. A. M. Brand
Enchanteresse	Mons. Jules Elie
Festiva Maxima	Philippe Rivoire
Kelway's Glorious	Sarah K. Thurlow
Lady Alexander Duff	Thomas C. Thurlow

Papaver nudicaule (Iceland Poppy)
Phlox
- Antonin Mercier
- Beacon
- Elizabeth Campbell
- Fireglow
- Marie Louise
- Miss Lingard
- Mrs. Jenkins
- Thor

Primula vulgaris (English Primrose)
Thymus citriodorus (Lemon Thyme) aromatic leaf
Valeriana officinalis (Garden Heliotrope)
Viola blanda (Sweet violets)
- *canadensis*
- *odorata*
- *pedata*
- *rosina*

Viola cornuta (Viola or Tufted Pansy)

VI

Drought and Heat-Resistant Perennials

Achillea eupatorium (Yarrow)
Aster (Michaelmas Daisy)
Betonica (Betony)
Chrysanthemum
- Warrior

Coreopsis grandiflora (Tickseed)
Dianthus barbatus (Sweet William)
Gaillardia (Blanket Flower)
Gypsophila (Babysbreath)
Helianthus (Perennial Sunflower)
Iris, Bearded
Nepeta (Catmint)
Oenothera missouriensis (Evening Primrose)

Papaver
 nudicaule (Iceland)
 orientale (oriental)
Rudbeckia (Coneflower)
Silene maritima (Catchfly)
Statice latifolia (Sea Lavender)
Valeriana (Garden Heliotrope)
Veronica (Speedwell)
Yucca filamentosa

VII

Seashore Hardies

High winds, salt spray and sandy soil epitomize the problems of seashore gardening. Without a tall screen, like a hedge of beach plum, bay or Japanese honeysuckle and considerable and repeated additions of humus and manure to the soil, few perennials will thrive. When they do, however, they are of unusual size and brilliant color. If in winter lengths of burlap are fastened on uprights to make a temporary screen for well-mulched plants and if other untoward conditions are minimized, many perennials prove extremely tolerant. Patches of binding grass planted beyond the flower bed areas help to prevent shifting of soil.

Althaea rosea (Hollyhock)
Armeria (Sea Pink)
Aster (Michaelmas Daisy)
Campanula (Bellflower)
Centaurea candidissima (Dusty Miller)
Chrysanthemum maximum (Shasta Daisy)
Coronaria (Rose Campion)
Dianthus (Pinks)

Echinops (Globe Thistle)
Erigeron (Midsummer Daisy or Fleabane)
Eryngium (Sea Holly)
Gaillardia (Blanket Flower)
Hemerocallis (Daylily)
Heuchera (Coralbells)
Hibiscus (Mallow)
Iris, Bearded and Siberian
Linum (Flax)
Lythrum (Loosestrife)
Monarda (Beebalm)
Phlox subulata (Mountain Pink)
Physostegia (False Dragonhead)
Rudbeckia (Coneflower)
Sedum spectabile
Silene maritima (Catchfly)
Statice latifolia (Sea Lavender)
Veronica maritima or *V. longifolia subsessilis* (Speedwell)
Yucca

VIII

City Dwellers

Althaea rosea (Hollyhock)
Alyssum saxatile (Basket-of-gold)
Anchusa myosotidiflora (Forget-me-not Anchusa)
Aquilegia (Columbine)
Chrysanthemum
Convallaria majalis (Lily-of-the-Valley)
Dianthus barbatus (Sweet William)
Dicentra spectabilis (Bleedingheart)
Dictamnus fraxinella (Gas Plant)
Eupatorium coelestinum (Hardy Ageratum)
Gaillardia (Blanket Flower)

Gypsophila (Babysbreath)
Hemerocallis (Daylily)
Heuchera (Coralbells)
Hesperis matronalis (Sweet Rocket)
Hosta (Plantain Lily or *Funkia*)
Iberis sempervirens (Hardy Candytuft)
Iris, Bearded
Mertensia (Virginia Bluebell)
Monarda (Beebalm or Bergamot)
Phlox subulata (Moss Pink)
divaricata (Wild Sweet William)
Plumbago larpentae (Leadwort)
Platycodon (Chinese Bellflower)
Sedum spectabile
Sempervivum tectorum (Hen and Chickens)
Statice armeria (Common Thrift)
Tradescantia virginiana (Spider Plant)
Viola (Tufted Pansy)

IX

Gray-leaved *Plants for Blending*

Arabis alpina (Rockcress)
Artemisia, Silver King
Alyssum saxatile (Basket-of-Gold)
Bocconia cordata (Plume Poppy)
Centaurea candidissima (Dusty Miller)
Cerastium tomentosum (Snow-in-Summer)
Dianthus allwoodi (Garden Pinks)
plumarius (Grass Pink)
Hosta fortunei (Daylily)
sieboldiana

Salvia sclarea
Stachys lanata
Veronica incana (Woolly speedwell)

X

Pale and Scented, for the Moonlight Garden

On pleasant evenings from May to October, a garden planted with pale and scented flowers becomes a sanctuary from both heat and stress. Here in surroundings quiet and remote, the essential dignity of life again asserts itself as our thoughts rise above trivialities and our spirits are fortified by tranquility. Such a garden repays necessarily careful designing and selective planting. Let the background be hemlock, pine, and white lilac, the important shade tree an apple or flowering cherry and the perennials such kinds as these.

Varieties with marked fragrance are starred.

For May

* *Aquilegia chrysantha alba* (Columbine—to July)
* *Asperula odorata* (Woodruff)
* *Convallaria majalis* (Lily-of-the-Valley)
Hemerocallis
Iris
  Crystal Beauty
  Desert Gold
Paeonia
  * Duchesse de Nemours
  * *Festiva maxima*
* *Primula vulgaris* (English Primrose)
* *Viola blanda* (Sweet White Violet)
Viola, White Perfection (Tufted Pansy—to August)

For June

* *Astilbe*, Deutschland
Campanula medium, White (Canterbury Bells—into July)
Chrysanthemum maximum, Mt. Shasta (Shasta Daisy—November)
Delphinium (Larkspur—to November)
chinense album
Galahad
* *Dianthus*
caryophyllus (Carnations—July)
plumarius (Garden Pinks—September)
Dictamnus alba (Gas Plant—to July)
Digitalis purpurea alba (Foxglove—into July)
Gypsophila, Bristol Fairy (Babysbreath—to October)
* *Hesperis matronalis* (Sweet Rocket)
Hemerocallis Sovereign (Daylily)
Iris
Mount Washington
Venus de Milo
Lupinus polyphyllus alba (Lupine—to August)
* *Oenothera missouriensis* (Evening Primrose—August)
* *Paeonia*, Kelway's Glorious
Baroness Schroeder
* Enchanteresse
* *Phlox* (to October)
Mia Ruys
Miss Lingard
* *Valeriana officinalis alba* (Garden Heliotrope—July)
* *Yucca filamentosa* (Adam's Needle)

For July

Althaea rosea, White (Hollyhock—August)
Iris kaempferi, Gold Bound (Japanese Iris)

Hemerocallis (Daylily—August)
* Dauntless
* Patricia
Sonny
* *Phlox* (to October)
Marie Louise
Mrs. Jenkins
* *Platycodon grandiflorum album* (Balloon Flower—October)

For August

* *Hosta subcordata grandiflora* (August Lily—September)
* *Boltonia asteroides,* White

For September

* *Aster,* Mt. Everest
* *Chrysanthemum*
Hebe
Lavender Lady
Northern Lights
Silver Moon
Liatris, White Spire (Gayfeather)

❦ ❦

CALENDAR OF CHORES

JANUARY

"Sing a song of winter,
The world stops dead.
Under snowy cover lid,
Flowers lie abed."
COSMO MONKHOUSE.

Make a New Year's resolution to plan better and so to work less in your garden. If you attempted too much last year, cut this down. Gardens are not meant to be an endurance test but a joy.

Chrysanthemum. On warm unseasonable middays, lift the cold frame glass for short periods of ventilation.

Helleborus (Christmas and Lenten Rose). Cut generous bouquets from the white, pink and green *niger* plants. If you have *H. foetidus,* pick at least one handsome inflorescence.

Convallaria (Lily-of-the-valley). If you have an abundance of these lift a clump or two, pot them, gradually introduce to heat indoors and then to sun. This will result in fragrant flowering in the house.

Make the acquaintance of the perennials this month. Study first a general catalogue like Wayside Gardens' exceptionally well-illustrated one. Then as your interest develops, obtain and read a few special catalogues on peony, iris, chrysanthemum or poppy. Many catalogues are sent free on request. A fee is usually charged for the more richly illustrated ones. If you are an experienced gardener, select a trial few of the newer varieties in your favorite plant group.

Get your husband to make you some seed flats. A good easily-handled size is twelve by twelve inches.

FEBRUARY

"This is the time when bit by bit
The days begin to lengthen sweet
And every minute gained is joy."
KATHARINE TYNAN.

Chrysanthemum. Continue to ventilate frame for longer periods as weather permits.

Astilbe, Iberis, Primula, Dielytra (Bleedinghearts). Dig a clump of any of these some pleasant day, pot them and urge them with sunshine, water and warmth to put on an out-of-season show.

Work and rework your garden plans this month. It's a very pleasant fireside occupations.

Get your orders in early to insure prompt delivery of choice material. Remember to include, too, fertilizers, mulching material, stakes, plant ties, tools if you need them, and various oddments. It's so much easier to start equipped than to have to await some necessary item just when you need it most. Order your "sundries" as locally as possible to save delivery costs but buy your plants where the exact variety you want is obtainable. Substitutions are seldom satisfactory to the particular gardener, especially when it's a matter of color.

Don't overlook the season's novelties but don't go all out for them either. The acquaintance of a few each year makes gardening that much more interesting.

Save your wood ashes. Either add them to the compost pit where they will speed decomposition or collect them until spring when, scattered on the garden, they will supply potash. To keep their fertilizing value intact, place them under cover. You want them "unleached" that is, unweathered.

MARCH

"The Robin is the one
That interrupts the morn
With hurried few express reports
When March is scarcely on."
EMILY DICKINSON.

Chrysanthemum. When you discover green leaves under the mulch in the cold frame, remove the mulch and the cold frame shade. But keep the glass down except during the warm part of the day.

Iris. Examine these and other perennials for signs of heaving. Particularly if your garden has not been mulched, will you need to go over plantings and firm back roots dislodged by frost.

Late this month poke around a bit and see what goes

on under the winter mulch. If green growth appears, loosen mulches to aerate plants. It's not time yet for removal unless the season is unusually advanced.

Try leading your husband's spring fever urge into cold frame building.

APRIL

> *"Sang the sunrise on an amber morn—*
> *'Earth be glad! An April day is born.*
> *Winter's done, and April's in the skies*
> *Earth, look up with laughter in your eyes!' "*
> CHARLES G. D. ROBERTS.

Iris. Clean plantings out by hand as early as possible. Burn old leaves and all debris in which may lie the eggs of the iris borer.

Dianthus chinensis (Chinese Pinks). Thin out plantings made last year.

Peony. If previously buds have blackened, dust with bordeaux mixture when plants are dewy to deter possible botrytis blight. Repeat dustings until buds appear. Set the double tripod supports around the plants before heavy growth makes the task a real chore. Apply a trowelful of wood ashes and one of sheep manure. Triple these amounts for enormous plants.

Chrysanthemum. Lift all but the cushion varieties (divide these in alternate years), discard centers and plant fresh single-rooted sections at distances depending on size. Space plants two-thirds their height apart is a good old rule. This means twelve to eighteen inches.

About the first of the month let the glass over the cold frame plants stay open all day and then at night too, as weather permits. Return separated stock to garden outside as growth develops.

Hardy Asters. Lift all plants. Discard woody centers. Plant three young, well-rooted shoots together to form a new clump. Provide fresh soil with bone meal or select a new site.

Daisies. Divide helenium and shasta the second year into many small sections which will equal the parent in one growing season.

Hardy Aster. Divide without fail each spring.

Campanula medium and calycantha (Canterbury Bell). Transplant to border quarters before buds set.

Delphinium. Fertilize established plants. Transfer youngsters from cold frame to permanent quarters early this month.

Cheiranthus allioni (Siberian Wallflower). Transplant to border as soon as bulbs and other early plants are far enough along to permit safe placement among them.

Viola cornuta. Sow this biennial now. It does not care for summer heat.

Remove the greater part of the winter mulch when forsythia blooms. Clean up the remainder or work it into the soil as buds appear on maple trees.

About mid-month apply to all established perennials a balanced commercial plant food in sufficient quantity slightly to obscure the soil. Rake in lightly and water well.

Set dry twiggy growth cut from privet or other shrubby material among low-branching perennials like achillea, gaillardia, coreopsis etc. These will soon hide their excellent supports.

On the 1st and 15th, dust or spray as is required to deter pests or disease.

Divide fall-flowering perennials at this time.

Scatter your hoard of wood ashes lightly over the perennial beds in any available amount.

In the cutting garden allow at least one row there for flowers for the altar. Chrysanthemums Avalanche, Algonquin and Winsome would be a lovely white, yellow and pink contribution.

MAY

"Now the bright morning star, day's harbinger
Comes dancing from the East, and leads with her
The flowery May, who from her green lap throws
The yellow cowslip and the pale primrose."

JOHN MILTON.

Iris. Make the acquaintance of Siberians and intermediates. They are worth knowing. If the season is dry, give all iris plantings a thorough soaking to improve flower quality. If last year borers attacked, dust dewy plants now with pyrethrum or rotenone and sulphur. Cut off any punctured leaves well below noticeable points of attack. Burn these and any debris around plantings.

Peony. Remove the side buds from each group of three if size rather than quantity is your aim. Otherwise let them all develop. Don't worry over the harmless ants on the buds.

Delphinium. Stake your fast-growing plants before a storm breaks off the lovely spires. They look well with a separate support for each flower stalk.

Phlox. To achieve unusual size, pinch out all but five stems of each mature clump.

Chrysanthemum. When divided single plants have six leaves, pinch out the tops to induce branching. Pinch back branches as each of these develops six leaves.

Late this month or early next, make sowings of spring-flowering perennials for next spring's bloom—arabis, alyssum, columbine, forget-me-not, iberis and primrose.

Around the 15th, apply the second dose of balanced plant food to all established perennials.

On the 1st and 15th, dust or spray as required.

If you are considering changes which must wait until fall, write yourself a garden note or two and tuck it into the appropriate spot. I use the broad topped Perfect Labels for this. In September I find such reminders to myself as "Move these hollyhocks to roomier quarters" or "Don't dig here. Remember your mertensia" or "This salmon phlox requests paler companions." It's a useful scheme.

If bleedinghearts are to be divided, mark them now so you can locate them later when they have died down and disappeared.

Keep notes of any color clashes. Later you can improve the situation perhaps by introducing some gray-foliaged plants among the offenders.

JUNE

"To him who in the love of Nature holds
Communion with her visible forms, she speaks
A various language."

WILLIAM CULLEN BRYANT.

Iris. Remove at the ground line all stalks carrying faded flowers. Keep orientals well soaked. Hand-weed clumps as they require. Make a list of any new iris you have seen this year and want next.

Iberis (Hardy Candytuft). Prune plants back after flowering to induce thick new growth.

Chrysanthemum. Place the tripod supports no longer needed by the peonies around the tall, huskier varieties. Fertilize lightly the middle of the month. Keep pinching side growth back.

Althaea (Hollyhock). Apply deterrent in Japanese beetle infested areas. Perhaps it would be better for you to omit hollyhocks for a few years.

Dianthus chinensis (Chinese Pinks). Sow these, if you have time, the third week.

Aquilegia (Columbine). Sow seeds every other year. Try Crimson Star or A. *flabellata nana alba* for a change.

Edging Plants. Take stem cuttings of rockcress, hardy candytuft, dwarf phlox, pinks, etc. when second growth starts. Also, consider, are the edges of your garden fine enough or should they be improved?

Peony. Select new varieties while they are in flower but delay planting until autumn.

Phlox. Be prompt about snipping off faded flowers.

Then you will have a long blooming season and no unwanted seedlings.

Hardy Asters. To keep them tractable in the border, pinch out all but three to four shoots in each clump.

Campanula medium and calycantha (Canterbury Bells). Sow late this month, preferably in a cold frame.

Digitalis (Foxglove). Sow thinly this month, preferably in a frame.

Dianthus barbatus (Sweet William). Sow this month in an open but protected seed bed or in a frame.

Apply a summer mulch to the border to discourage weeds and conserve moisture. This is especially good for delphinium and anemones.

Fork over the material in your compost pit and soak it with a slow-running hose for a whole day.

On the 1st and 15th, dust or spray your perennials as they require.

Sow now for early summer bloom next year, seeds of perennial coralbells, lupines, pinks, meadowrue, thermopsis, and pyrethrum.

JULY

"A something in a summer's day
As slow her flambeaux burn away,
Which solemnizes me."

EMILY DICKINSON.

If the weather is very hot, don't read this for a while.

Just sit and fan. Remember, gardening is primarily for fun. Doubtless your borders can survive a little neglect at this time.

Iberis (Hardy Candytuft). Be regular about dusting this month especially if the humidity is high. You won't see the red spider but a yellow plant usually means he's been seriously at work on his favorite. Forceful hose sprays directed from below break webs. Sulphur scattered on soil on a hot day fumigates the spider away.

Phlox. Dust for red spider and mildew and give deep soakings if there is little rain.

Linum (Flax). Remove at ground line some of the hardening older shoots which have flowered freely. This will induce new growth.

Althaea. (Hollyhock). Watch out for red spider and rust. Use sulphur as a deterrent.

Helleborus (Christmas or Lenten Rose). A few deep summer soakings are to its liking through dry spells.

Chrysanthemum. Guard against mildew by dusting and soak if there is drought. Fertilize mid-month. Stop pinching back early varieties by the 15th, later ones by the 30th.

Hemerocallis and Hosta (Daylily). Water well in dry weather or bloom may be meager.

Delphinium. If the weather is damp and muggy, be faithful about dusting to deter mildew and blight. Don't let annuals crowd these plants when they are cut back and small after flowering. Allow a two weeks' rest after flowering, then fertilize.

Biennials. Many of them can be sown late this month or early next. Time this for a cool spell after a rain.

Hardy Asters. Stake early, particularly if you are allowing only a few tall shoots for each plant.

Cheiranthus allioni (Siberian Wallflower). Sow now.

Viola. Cut back sharply, water deeply and mulch. Maybe they will prove perennial for you.

Fork over the compost pit and soak it well.

If the weather is dry, soak sections of the garden thoroughly and progressively until each has been moistened six inches deep. Use the overhead sprinkler, only occasionally and never at night, to cleanse and refresh plant tops.

On the 1st and 15th, dust or spray as required. Aim to deter rather than to eradicate. It's easier and cheaper. This is a bad pest and disease month, especially if the weather is muggy.

Protect the corners of your garden from careless steps or a dragging hose by short right-angle sections of twelve-inch wire fencing. The hardware man will cut them to your specification. These short bits of fencing also help in the re-education of dogs and children whose short cut habits need changing.

AUGUST

"A Husband is the sort of man,
Who tries to help you all he can;
But, somehow, never quite succeeds,
In doing what the garden needs."

REGINALD ARKELL.

Iris. If foliage rots at base, lift plants, cut decay from rhizomes, dust with sulphur, expose to sun for a few days and reset in a new location or in fresh soil.

Aconite. Keep well soaked.

Chrysanthemum. Soak deeply if rainfall is slight. This will help check leaf browning. Stake as growth indicates. Three bamboo lengths bound by green raffia will do a neat job.

Phlox. Increase your supply by taking stem cuttings of some favorite varieties. Cut two-thirds back those which have bloomed heavily. They will soon get to work again.

Delphinium. Sow fresh seed (shaken up with Semesan) some cool day this month. Use a deep flat and keep it in a cool garage or shed.

Lupine. Late this month wake up your resting plants with a good deep watering and a light application of some balanced fertilizer.

Althaea (Hollyhock). Sow now.

Hardy Asters. Don't let them suffer drought.

Helleborus (Christmas or Lenten Rose). How about making a planting of these this month or next? They will complete your flowering year.

Edging Plants. Consider sowing mixed *Dianthus plumarius* for a large supply of fragrant edging plants.

Digitalis (Foxglove). Space six-week-old June-sown plants ten inches apart in row or cold frame. Be careful they do not suffer dryness.

Viola tricolor (Pansy). Sow late this month for a big crop but they are good biennials to buy.

After a rain, during a relatively cool spell sow seeds of the summer and fall-flowering perennials—aconite, gaillardia, platycodon, salvia, scabiosa and shasta daisy and stokesia.

Turn over and soak the compost pit once this month. On the 1st and 15th, dust or spray again. It's boring but still very important.

Take root cuttings this month or next of bleeding-hearts, babysbreath, anemone, phlox, statice and oriental poppy.

SEPTEMBER

"O sweet September! thy first breezes bring
The dry leaf's rustle and the squirrel's laughter,
The cool, fresh air, whence health and vigor spring,
And promise of exceeding joy hereafter."

GEORGE ARNOLD.

Iris. Divide and reset crowded clumps. Cut tops half way back. Plant small divisions of bearded varieties one inch deep and fifteen inches apart. Face rhizomes in the same direction. Set three single pieces of Siberians three inches apart to form one clump. Water regularly if dry weather follows transplanting.

Biennials. Transfer open sowings to rows in a protected reserve bed. Separate cold frame seedlings to stand four to eight inches apart, according to variety.

Primrose. Separate into small but not too tiny divisions or it will disappear.

Anemone. Don't be alarmed if your first year plants aren't flowering much. They incline to be backward about coming forward until they are well established in your garden.

Phlox. About every third or fourth year divide big clumps into thirds.

Peony. Divide and reset any failing old plants or set out new ones the last two weeks this month. Remember a place in the sun, good drainage and only two to three inches of soil over the crowns.

Oriental Poppy. Set out new plants and divide and reset over thick old ones. You can also take root cuttings now.

Delphinium. Place your new seedlings four inches apart in a cold frame. Use equal thirds leaf mold, top soil and sand.

Aconite. If well-watered plants begin to curl and droop, suspect verticillum wilt. All you can do is discard and burn them. But be sure first that dryness has not produced this sickly appearance.

Chrysanthemum. If you wish to transfer well budded plants to the border, wait for cloudy weather. Then soak plants the day before and several days after moving. They will bloom on without an indication of resentment. Stake any inclined to be floppy.

Heuchera (Coralbells). Perhaps you can edge a whole bed by dividing several of your large established clumps. Separate by pulling gently apart. Cut from the tap root only sections with some fine roots of their own.

Cheiranthus allioni (Siberian Wallflower). Transplant seedlings to a reserve row.

If you haven't one already, prepare a pit in which to start composting autumn leaves. Two by four by three feet will hold a wonderful supply of humus. Over each twelve-inch layer of leaves or other vegetable matter scatter lime or Adco and a thin layer of soil or sand. Leave a hollow at the top to catch the rain. By spring some of this mixture will be sufficiently decomposed for use. And it is marvelous stuff.

On the 1st and 15th, give final dustings or sprayings but don't put your apparatus in storage yet. You might be unlucky enough to have to use it again. But it isn't likely.

By all means build a cold frame in which to sow seeds early and winter many plants safely.

Any time now you can deal with the spring-flowering perennials which require dividing or transplanting.

If your order of lily bulbs has not come, place stakes among your perennials to indicate proper bulb placement. When some lilies are already present but there are others yet to go in, perhaps next month, mark present locations with wire stakes and future ones with bamboo. Stakes left in place over winter are also a safe guide to early cultivation of perennials, if late hardy plants or bulbs must be worked around.

OCTOBER

"Where are the songs of spring? Aye, where are they?
Think not of them, thou hast thy music, too."

JOHN KEATS.

Peony. Cut off and burn all foliage. Work in a trowelful of bone meal per plant.

Chrysanthemum. As soon as flowering ceases, cut back tops and lift stock plants of doubtfully hardy varieties.

Place these in an open cold frame and water once a week until a hard freeze occurs.

Visit a chrysanthemum nursery or any fair-sized private collection and make your list of varieties for next year. (Forgive me, please, for making so many notes on chrysanthemums. They're my favorite perennials.)

If you plan to mulch the borders with leaves, collect in a corner of the shrubbery border or in baskets, all you will need of the type which curl when they fall—oak, birch, beech, hardwood maple, etc. Avoid soggy mulches made by poplar or Norway maple.

Should there be little rainfall this month, as sometimes occurs, soak your perennials finally and deeply about the third week. Plants which have suffered drought incline to winterkill. Let yours go dormant in good condition.

Early this month is a grand time to redo a badly designed perennial border or one overcrowded by the maturity of its plants. Sometimes I do sections year by year —edging and foreground one autumn, center or rear another. Lift out all plants. Separate those requiring it. Throw away poor varieties or those past their prime. Dig deeply. Work compost and bone meal into the soil. Reset plants. The weather usually favors you and the work is fun. Ensuing satisfaction, tremendous!

NOVEMBER

"Shed no tear! O, shed no tear!
The flower will bloom another year.
Weep no more! O, weep no more!
Young buds sleep in the root's white core."
JOHN KEATS.

Iris. After a hard freeze, mulch new plantings lightly the first year. Only in subzero sections continue this practice in subsequent years.

Chrysanthemum. After freezing weather, mulch all except de Petris varieties. After mulching those in the frame put down the glass and shade it. You may not need to do this until next month.

Helleborus (Christmas or Lenten Rose). Examine them early this month. Enough flowers may be open for a first bouquet. Think twice about cutting the evergreen foliage of the variety *niger.* Add bone meal lightly any time now and a thin layer of compost.

Early this month, mulch lightly all young plants just beyond the seedling stage. Do not cover adults until after the first hard freeze.

Plant inconspicuously a few bushes of California privet as a source of neat twiggy supports for coreopsis, gaillardia, veronica, etc.

DECEMBER

"December drops no weak, relenting tear,
By our fond summer sympathies ensnared,
Nor from the perfect circle of the year
Can even Winter's crystal gems be spared."
CHRISTOPHER P. CRANCH.

Helleborus. Cut these flowers freely for pleasing arrangements with evergreens. When they fade, try a very hot water dip, followed by a cold steeping. This may revive them for your further pleasure.

Iris stylosa. Care for and ventilate this one in the cold frame. And don't be discouraged if flowers do not appear until the second or third year of residence.

After the first hard freeze—not simply a touch of frost—mulch perennials to keep them cold and unstimulated by occasional midwinter warmth. Pull the mulching material under not over green-topped plants. After the first year leave uncovered peonies, iris, oriental poppies and delphinium (except in very cold sections). Daylilies never need a cover.

For your garden-mad friends remember that an order for some choice perennial plants is a very fine present.

Merry Christmas and Good Gardening next year!

SOURCES OF MATERIAL

Through years of gardening each of us comes to depend on certain firms to supply our needs and to keep us informed of worth-while improvements through interesting catalogues or special plant lists. This is by no means a complete index to the materials of fine plantsmen. It is simply a first plant guide for you who do not yet have your own favorite and ready sources of supply. For seeds, fertilizers, and plant stakes, etc., apply to your nearest seed store:

Betscher, C., Dover, O. (Hemerocallis)
Bobbink & Atkins, East Rutherford, N. J. (General)
Brand Peony Farms, 134 East Division St., Faribault, Minn.
Bristol Nurseries, Bristol, Conn. (Chrysanthemums, etc.)
Carroll Gardens, Westminster, Md. (General)
Cooley's Iris Gardens, Silverton, Ore.
Fairmount Gardens, 166 Fairmount St., Lowell, Mass. (Iris, Poppies, Hemerocallis and Hosta)
Farr Nursery Co., Weiser Park, Pa. (Hemerocallis, etc.)
Fasel, Isabel B., R. D. 1, Westchester, Pa. (Hellebores)

Flowerfield Bulb Farm, Flowerfield, L. I., N. Y. (Oriental Iris, etc.)

Hoodacres Originating Gardens, Troutdale, Ore. (Delphinium)

Jackson & Perkins Co., Newark, N. Y. (General)

The Liebenthaler Co., 300 Catalpa Drive, Dayton, O. (Oriental Poppies)

National Iris Gardens, Beaverton, Ore.

Oberlin Peony Gardens, Sinking Spring, Pa.

Pearce, Rex D., Moorestown, N. J. (Many rare items)

Salbach Gardens, 644 Woodmont Ave., Berkeley, Cal. (Iris)

Wayside Gardens, Mentor, O. (General)

Zager, H. A., 4215 Urbandale Ave., Des Moines, I. (Hemerocallis and Hosta)

GLOSSARY

Aeration. This is the air content of the soil. One of the reasons for frequent cultivation of a flower bed is to increase the healthful circulation of air in the soil.

Annuals. Their life cycle is completed in one year during which they develop from seed, flower, form seed and die. Some like tobacco and cornflower are said to self-sow, that is, their seed survives the cold and germinates the next year.

Anther. Some flowers like the single peonies reveal prominent little sacs, or anthers, borne on long threads in the center of the blossom. When the cells mature they release golden pollen grains.

Biennials. These come to perfection in the course of two years. The first year the plants develop. The second the flowers appear, and if permitted, the seeds. Then the plants may as well be discarded.

Cambium. Just beneath the bark of tree or shrub lies a layer of living tissue. This is the cambium. When trees are cut down their probable age can be determined by a count of the annual rings of cambium tissue.

Cold frame. This basically is a box with a bed of soil for the bottom and a piece of glass for the top. Inserted in the soil in a sunny place it is so set that the front is about ten inches high and the rear twenty. This provides a sloping surface to catch the sunshine.

Corm. This is a short, fleshy, erect, underground stem with scale-like leaves surrounding it. The gladiolus grows from a corm which is often incorrectly called a bulb.

Flat. This is a shallow box in which seeds are sown or seedlings transplanted. The usual size is sixteen by twenty-two and one-half inches with a two- to four-inch depth. Bottom boards are separated one-quarter inch to permit drainage. If makeshift flats of cigar boxes are used a few half-inch holes are bored in the bottom so that excess water may escape.

Floret. The individual small flowers which make up a thick flower cluster are called florets. They are plainly seen in the make-up of phlox or delphinium.

Germination. When seeds start to grow into little plants, we say germination has taken place.

Head. A dense flower cluster like that of the chrysanthemum is called a head.

Hybrid. An individual resulting from the crossing of two species or of two parents which differ basically in some strongly marked characteristic. Our handsomest delphiniums are the results of such cross fertilization.

Inflorescence. The arrangement of flowers on a plant, the type of its cluster, is its inflorescence. These may be in heads, racemes, panicles, spikes, etc. Sometimes the word is also used to indicate the manner of its opening.

Naturalize. To plant informally in drifts or colonize to simulate nature's own self-sowing is to naturalize.

Organic Material. This was once living matter as contrasted with non-living or inorganic matter. Manures, rotted leaves or compost and bone meal are organic fertilizers while commercial fertilizers are largely chemical or inorganic.

Panicle. A loose spire-like flower form such as the astilbe or spirea and phlox produce is called a panicle.

Perennials. These are root hardy plants which die down after frost but green up again each spring and flower seasonally for a period of more than two years.

pH. This is a term describing the sweet-sour condition of the soil the way Fahrenheit readings indicate hot-cold degrees of temperature. Most perennials thrive in a fairly neutral or pH7 soil with toleration for slight variations either way.

Raceme. A slender elongated flower cluster in which each small flower is borne on a little stalk of its own is a raceme. The bleedingheart and lily-of-the-valley are examples.

Rhizome. An underground stem, usually thicker than the visible stem, with joints from which roots grow is a rhizome. Bearded iris has typical rhizomes.

Species. This is something nature produces. It is a group of plants sharing certain distinctive characteristics which indicate a common parent or genus. In a plant name the first word indicates the genus, the second the species it belongs to, the third the variety as *Phlox paniculata,* Miss Lingard.

Specimen Plant. A plant grown by itself or prominently placed is often so described.

Stock Plant. A plant used to increase one's supply or

saved for this purpose is called a stock plant. The tender chrysanthemum wintered in the cold frame for propagating in the spring is a stock plant.

Taproot. That long thick root which babysbreath, oriental poppy and lupine develop is such a one. Plants with this type root system require extra care in transplanting so as not to injure this main root.

Variety. The slight variations within a species which are noticeable but not important enough to constitute another species are called varieties.

Lath Shade. This is a screen to protect soil and plants from direct sunlight. It is frequently made by nailing plaster lath to a light board frame.

Spike. A slim elongated flower cluster in which individual flowers grow without stalks and close to the main stalk is a spike. Gayfeather, delphinium and lupine are typical spike flowers.

INDEX

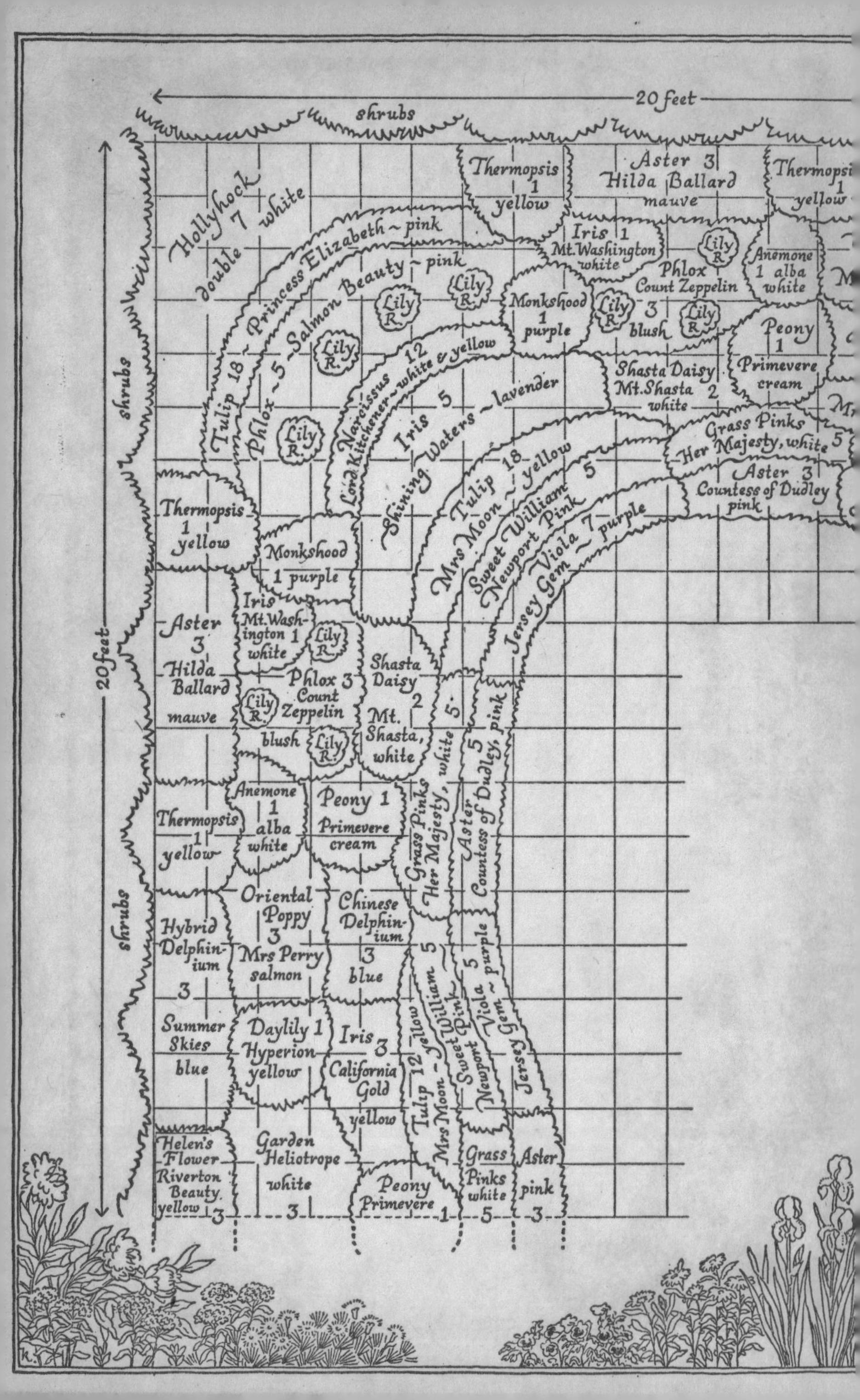

20 feet
shrubs
20 feet
shrubs
shrubs
Hollyhock double 7 white
Thermopsis 1 yellow
Aster 3 Hilda Ballard mauve
Thermopsi 1 yellow
Tulip 18 ~ Princess Elizabeth ~ pink
Phlox ~ 5 ~ Salmon Beauty ~ pink
Lily R.
Iris 1 Mt. Washington white
Phlox Count Zeppelin 3 blush
Anemone 1 alba white
Monkshood 1 purple
Peony 1 Primevere cream
Narcissus 12 Lord Kitchener ~ white & yellow
Iris 5 Shining Waters ~ lavender
Shasta Daisy Mt. Shasta 2 white
Grass Pinks Her Majesty, white 5
Aster 3 Countess of Dudley pink
Mrs Moon Tulip 18 ~ yellow
Sweet William 5 Newport Pink
Jersey Gem Viola 7 ~ purple
Thermopsis 1 yellow
Monkshood 1 purple
Aster 3 Hilda Ballard mauve
Iris Mt. Washington 1 white
Phlox 3 Count Zeppelin blush
Shasta Daisy 2 Mt. Shasta, white
Thermopsis 1 yellow
Anemone 1 alba white
Peony 1 Primevere cream
Grass Pinks Her Majesty, white 5
Aster 5 Countess of Dudley, pink
Hybrid Delphinium 3
Oriental Poppy 3 Mrs Perry salmon
Chinese Delphinium 3 blue
Summer Skies blue
Daylily 1 Hyperion yellow
Iris 3 California Gold yellow
Tulip 12 Mrs Moon ~ yellow
Sweet William 5 Newport Pink
Viola 5 Jersey Gem ~ purple
Helen's Flower Riverton Beauty yellow 3
Garden Heliotrope white 3
Peony Primevere 1
Grass Pinks white 5
Aster pink 3